HT
115
S2

Saalman, Howard.

Medieval cities

29760-2

DATE		
NO	Newer	3/2012

MEDIEVAL CITIES

PLANNING AND CITIES

PLANNING AND CITIES

General Editor

GEORGE R. COLLINS, Columbia University

MEDIEVAL CITIES

HOWARD SAALMAN

GEORGE BRAZILLER   NEW YORK

CONTENTS

GENERAL EDITOR'S PREFACE

The history of cities, of their physical planning, and of man's theories of urbanism represents a facet of cultural history that is particularly meaningful to us in these years of world-wide urban crisis. Clearly, the dimensions and variety of problems that face us as citizens today are infinitely greater than those of any previous civilization. Nevertheless, it is illuminating for us to examine town structures and ideals of other times and places and to determine how they related to the functioning of the society that was being housed.

It is our hope in this series of books to treat many aspects of urban history and to do so efficiently and in depth by inviting a specialist for each volume who can enlighten us from the vantage point of his own field of competence and his personal enthusiasm for it. We have therefore divided the many titles of our intended survey into a number of categories, such as epochs and areas, theories and models, great planners, and so forth. We have urged our authors to dwell especially on the structural, architectural, and formal components of their subject, not only because these factors seem to be disregarded in the precipitate growth of contemporary cities, but also because the literature on these features of urban history is not at the moment easily accessible to students and interested laymen.

We are commencing with books about epochs and areas. In this historical overview we will range from the root beginnings of the process of urbanism, as seen in settlement patterns of "primitive" man and in the rebirth of towns in Europe during the Middle Ages, to the most sophisticated formulae of baroque despots and of contemporary systems analysts.

G.R.C.

PREFACE

This volume is not a survey of medieval cities. It does not attempt to trace the history of medieval cities from their embryonic origins to their full development nor to define all the sources of their components. What is essayed here is a critical look at what a medieval city is or was, at the structures and spaces which were its characteristic components, and at the economic, social and political forces which gave this complex its shape. I have emphasized not the infinite diversity which distinguishes one town from the other, but the general features which medieval cities have in common. The problems of origins and the early evolution of the towns (in the embryonic stages) are too complex for brief treatment. Islamic cities will be treated in another volume in this series. The problem of ideal cities raises questions which fall outside the scope of this volume.

The author wishes to express his appreciation to the publisher and general editor for their invaluable assistance with the illustrations for this volume.

H.S.

Carnegie-Mellon University
Pittsburgh, Pennsylvania

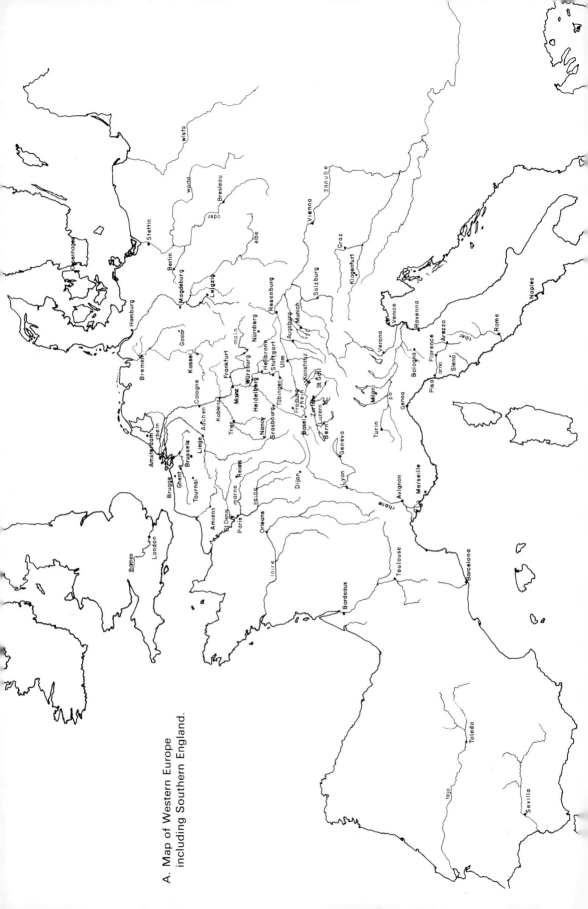

A. Map of Western Europe including Southern England.

DEFINITION

A city is a tool for the production and exchange of goods and services. A city may also be a place where people live, study, play, worship, or have children. It may be a place of magic or of terror, of beauty or of ugliness. But such things are true of other places as well, fields, mountaintops or caves—and such attributes are subjective and secondary to the essential function of a city.

Incomprehension of the fundamental nature and use of cities leads inevitably to a misunderstanding of medieval cities. For example, it has been remarked that medieval cities had irregular, badly lit streets, that there were no trees or parks, that they were overcrowded and unsanitary; in short, not "good places to live." On the other hand, such characteristics have also been considered "charming," "colorful" or "romantic." All of this is superbly beside the point. It could be argued that these qualities made the medieval city a better instrument for performing its primary function, the production and exchange of goods and services. It is not our concern to judge the medieval city; let us try to understand it! The fact that the best known and the best functioning medieval cities were crowded only proves that they were successful. There is only one criterion of failure for cities: depopulation.

BACKGROUND

The pattern of renewed urbanization and industrialization in tenth and eleventh century Western Europe can be better evaluated when compared with similar processes in the Mediterranean basin, which began in the sixth century B. C. and reached their climax in the cities of the Roman Imperial period. Industrialization, it should be said, is not synonymous with mechanization. It *does* imply an organized process of production and distribution of goods and services—and a genius for order and organization was the very basis of the Roman state. Everything from fun to funerals found its place in the legally and traditionally ordered scheme of things and—up to a point—everything worked well. If mechanization remained relatively limited it was because cheap and slave labor provided the required substitute, as in the American south of the early nineteenth century. No project the Romans undertook failed because of inadequate technology.

The Romans were imperialists long before they had emperors. The empire consisted of urban units connected by a system of efficient roads and bridges. (Many of these roads and bridges are still in use.) The production and exchange of goods and services can take place only within a framework of order founded on justice. Laws guaranteeing justice find their rationale in a broader conception of a divinely ordered universe. The heart of Hellenistic and Roman cities was the forum (Figs. 1, 2), which was flanked by both law courts and temples. Religious and secular life were no more separable in antiquity than in the Middle Ages.

The Romans enjoyed their country villas and romanticized the rural idyll of Homeric times. But the land between their cities was rationalized by division into one-hundred-foot square units and farmed with an efficiency that can only be labeled "industrialized agriculture." With the masses of population concentrated in the large cities throughout the empire, less effective means of food production, of overseas and overland transportation, of agricultural products, or of less highly developed port facilities and storage terminals were practically unthinkable. With the satisfaction of basic needs and growing prosperity came a growing demand for manufactured products of all kinds. Roman craftsmen were prepared to make, and Roman merchants were ready to distribute, an impressive variety of products which gave life in urban apartments and rural homes a standard which compares favorably with later centuries. Architecture and engineering—utilizing stone, brick, and concrete masonry as well as metal, wood, and glass—achieved a level of accomplishment by which all conceivable needs from those of frontier camps to those of town palaces could be and were met. The scale and quality of Roman public building and engineering have never been equalled.

While the cult of the ancient gods formed the basis of Roman conceptions of law and order, a tolerance of a variety of cultures, languages, and religions within the empire gave the total social and political structure a flexibility which ensured its long existence. A town like Dura-Europos (Fig. 3) on the periphery of the empire had room not only for a temple of Jupiter (Zeus), on its forum, but for a variety of cult buildings of numerous western and oriental mystery religions including a Christian meeting house and a synagogue. If these latter found their place in the less prosperous and less desirable quarters near the town walls, they were nevertheless within the pale.

But the key to a workable and durable urban civilization is a social and political system in which human passions and economic pressures can be brought into a reasonably stable equilibrium. The Roman state had no magic solution to this explosive problem of all highly developed societies. However, aside from a magnificently organized army and an efficient bureaucracy, the state did have escape valves for social pressures. Bread, circuses, and army careers provided an outlet for the masses; the theaters, the baths, the prospects of a good position in the state services and a pleasant retirement in the country or at a shore resort appeased the ambitions of the middle and upper classes. The tolerated mystery religions offered succor to the hopeless. All of this complex culture and its variegated architecture found room and place within the framework of the ancient city, making possible its primary economic function without which all else had neither mode nor means.

It might be said that the degree of integrated urbanization achieved in the Roman Imperial period has not again been reached in the long cycle of urbanization which began anew in the tenth and eleventh centuries after a long decline, and which still continues. True, the mechanization of production and transport has reached levels in the past one hundred and fifty years of which the Romans or the people of the Middle Ages may not even have dreamed. But to repeat, mechanization is not a true index of urbanization.

State and religion, workers and managers, businessmen and bureaucrats, city and country, open space and built-up space, and the sheer variety of trained human beings necessary for a complex of functions must be in reasonable balance if the city is to be an effective tool in an ordered and industrialized society. In this respect the process of urbanization reinitiated some nine hundred years ago has yet to attain the level of efficiency of Imperial Rome at its peak.

CAROLINGIAN INTERLUDE

Henri Pirenne attributed the decline of Roman urban civilization not to the triumph of Christianity or the impact of foreign and barbarian invasions, but to the gradual throttling of Mediterranean trade resulting from the advance of Islam in the seventh century. His contemporary, Alfons Dopsch, argued that the "barbarians" had not been all that uncivilized to start with, and that Roman civilization continued in a minor key after the invasions. But Dopsch felt that the Carolingian age marked a great new beginning rather than a sharp decline. Social and economic historians in recent decades, spurred by these conflicting views, have uncovered new evidence and offered more moderate interpretations.[1]

Trade and urban life along the main waterways never died out during the Carolingian period, particularly in the old Roman cities of western Europe. Nor was the Mediterranean ever completely closed to enterprising merchants traveling in convoys to trade for precious Eastern goods with Christian, Jew, and Moslem alike. Carolingian administrative, legal, and economic reforms were not anti-urban as such, and Carolingian ideals, expressed in art and architecture, comprised the vision of a reconstituted ancient grandeur. The Carolingians used the ancient cities as places of habitation, as fortified settlements from which to dominate the surrounding countryside. The surviving physical apparatus of the old towns, the walls and buildings, served because it already existed, a convenient legacy of an earlier age. Bishops and counts sat in them, repairing the walls as needed and building themselves forts and cathedrals. But the merchants' settlements, frequently outside the walls, were small. Manufacture and trade, supplying the courts, shrank to a minimum. The towns were no longer primarily places of production and exchange, but of consumption.

The gradual turn to consumption in the Italian cities, as production shifted to the East and to western Europe, had been a significant phenomenon in the gradual decline of the late Roman Empire. The increasing risks and costs of transporting agricultural goods and manufactures in the ensuing centuries led to increasing urban stagnation throughout western Europe as well. The advance of Islam in the Mediterranean basin aggravated an already advanced condition. The raids of the Norsemen in the ninth century did still further damage.[2]

An important Carolingian center such as Aachen was not a significant city in spite of the pseudo-antique paraphernalia of the imperial residence. Marginal production and exchange took place in the *Vicus* (small merchant's settlement) that grew up near the palace.[3] Its limited population catered to the immediate needs of the court and the small bureaucracy. Embassies from abroad and a few merchants commissioned by the court supplied items of luxury.

While the court ceremonial, court art, and the complex iconography of court-sponsored residences and monastic foundations wore a veneer of antique imitation, the liturgical nature of Carolingian churches differed profoundly from that of the Constantinian churches, which inspired aspects of their plans and elevations. While the great churches of Constantinian times marked the major sites of Christian tradition and martyrdom in the centers and around the periphery of the late antique world, the Carolingian buildings contained an encyclopedic collection of fragments from such sites and from the whole martyrology of saints, disposed in hieratically arranged altars.[4] This liturgical evolution has urban implications as well. The Constantinian sites implied pilgrimage, travel, a functioning system of roads, and a network of cities. The Carolingian churches bore testimony to the decline of travel, roads, cities, and of the trade which had been the lifeblood of a vanished world.

Nothing indicates more clearly the contrast between the urban precedents and the non-urban nature of Carolingian architectural phenomena than the famous Plan of St. Gall (Fig. 4). The elements of this composition can be traced to that most central of urban centers, the Forum of Trajan in Rome (Fig. 2). Cloister, chapter hall, church, and laboratoria derive directly from the great colonnaded square, the basilica, the temple, and the markets. Yet all the characteristics of a true city are missing. Some of the monastery production was for the market, but trading was carried out not in the monastery but in faraway markets, by commissioned traders.[5] Exchange among the members of the community was non-existent, trade with passing travelers minimal. It cannot even be said that the monastic scheme exemplified in the St. Gall parchment and embodied in numerous abbeys from the ninth century on, preserved the elements of the ancient city in capsule form until the time when the prerequisites for urban revival were again at hand. When that time came, the monasteries, mostly isolated in the countryside away from the major trade routes, played a minor role in the rebirth of cities, and few of them formed the nuclei of significant future towns.

The medieval cities we will examine here, while not totally unlike or uninfluenced by the tradition of the great ancient cities,[6] evolved their characteristic structure under changed social, political and economic conditions. The formal symmetries of Hellenistic-Roman derivation, preserved in the Plan of St. Gall and in the long line of medieval monasteries and cathedrals, found no echoes in urban design until the coming of a new age with new perspectives in the Renaissance.

ELEVENTH CENTURY BEGINNINGS

While a few towns along the Channel coast, such as Quentovic and Doorstad, were centers of sporadic overseas trade in the eighth, ninth, and tenth centuries, the Carolingian and early Ottonian age was a period of urban stagnation. The real centers of Carolingian cultural life and political and economic power were the great imperially sponsored monasteries in the old Frankish and the newly conquered Saxon and Lombard lands. It is a symptom of this trend that the abbeys of Saint-Denis, Sainte-Geneviève, and Saint-Germain-des-Prés were more important at this time than the nearby town of Paris.

By the middle of the eleventh century all this had changed. The Norsemen—who had made the North Sea, the Channel and inland waterways as dangerous in the eighth and early ninth centuries as the Moslems the Mediterranean—had settled down in Normandy, and laid the basis for one of the future great states of Europe with the conquest of Anglo-Saxon England in 1066. By this time, too, Norman knights were challenging Moslem pirates and Byzantine garrisons for control of the Italian coast on both the Tyrrhenian and the Adriatic sides. Militant adventurers out of the North had beaten trade routes into the heart of Western Russia. The expansive surge of Islam around the Mediterranean had slowed to a standstill, and Moslem dynasties from Persia to Spain were concerned more with internal consolidation and prosperity than with further conquest. The Byzantine Empire, not yet confronted by the Turkish menace, was in one of its recurring periods of resurgence. The social pressures created by the slow crumbling of the feudal system in western Europe found an outlet in the Crusades. Meanwhile, Constantinople attained new heights of prosperity as the hub of the movement between Europe and the Holy Land. Venice, Genoa, and Pisa made their maritime fortunes by capitalizing on the renascent international mobility. While successive dynasties of German kings continued to play the game of Holy Roman Empire with an increasingly powerful papacy in Rome, France, loosely united under Capetian rule, tended its fields and its fences and was wary of rule by either popes or Germans. Thus the Low Countries, as well as Italy, the North Sea and Baltic coasts and the Rhone, Rhine and Danube valleys of France and Germany, were the lands where trade and production for trade had the most favorable location and the most promising future. Here is where the towns, the essential tools for the production and exchange of goods and services, developed most quickly, shaped by the very process that made their appearance or reappearance inevitable.

PREMISES

The historical processes of socio-political evolution and mercantile expansion that mark the course of the eleventh and twelfth centuries, were naturally several paces ahead of the gradually developing urban centers that were to give them their architectural framework. It might even be said that when medieval cities finally attained something like their most perfect form, their high noon was already turning to twilight.

The historian concerned with medieval cities, moreover, is faced with a situation which does not confront the student of medieval political, social, and economic history. The political historian has his charters, his bulls, his records and chronicles. The social historian has a wealth of philosophical, religious and poetical literature, both courtly and popular, with which to conjure. The economic historian can begin where the others leave off, weighing his coins, deciphering bank records and even adding some occasional hard statistics to his bag of tricks. The art historian has no lack of illuminated manuscripts, reliquaries, ivories, and sculptured portals to fill his monographs, and the architectural historian has his churches. But the historian of medieval cities must begin with the admission that when he is dealing with medieval towns they are in the garb of the late fifteenth and sixteenth centuries at the very earliest. Rare indeed is the *Altstadt* that can boast a secular building older than the fifteenth century, and many are the *Vieux quartiers* dating almost wholly from the seventeenth century or even later. The quaint old "medieval" town idealized by Pugin in his *Contrasts* of 1836 has a decidedly Tudor flavor. The "Gothic" Strasbourg recalled by Goethe was that of the fifteenth to eighteenth centuries, and so it is with Ruskin's Venetian stones and the Wagnerian Nuremberg of Hans Sachs.

This is a distinction to be made with emphasis at the outset when dealing with even the best known "medieval" cities. It is the Renaissance butterfly we are looking at, not the medieval caterpillar. On the whole we have relatively little hard topographical knowledge concerning the medieval towns in their thirteenth, not to mention their twelfth or eleventh century states.[7] If this study does not deal with the "medieval house," it is because there are literally no medieval houses to discuss, aside from a few surviving thirteenth century towers.[8] The

20

earliest views of important centers like Florence, Paris, or Rome date from the late fifteenth and the first half of the sixteenth centuries, and some of these early views with their low bird's eye perspectives, invaluable as they are, furnish only limited information on actual street patterns. It is only in the time of Braun and Hogenberg, Mattheus Merian and Wenzel Hollar in the late sixteenth and seventeenth centuries that most of the "medieval" cities become subject to detailed topographical analysis (Amsterdam, Fig. 8). Conclusions based on such late evidence must be drawn with caution.

This understood, it may be said, on the other hand, that a study of medieval cities utilizing this material is not based on wholly false premises. Urban patterns, once established, changed only very gradually, if at all, before the middle of the nineteenth century. The location, shape, and scale of major public and religious buildings, of open and built-up areas, of bridges, walls and town gates, underwent a most gradual process of modification in the course of centuries. An examination of these urban patterns and their evolution is the subject of the following chapters.

FAUBOURGS

WALLS I

Tools are precious things. They are intrinsically valuable and useful on application. They must be protected against theft or destruction and against illegitimate use. Town walls served both of these functions. While one tends to think of them in terms of siege, with the militia behind the crenellations pouring boiling oil on ascending invaders (Coblenz, Fig. 6), the everyday and even more important purpose of the walls should not be neglected: control of entry and exit in peacetime. To accomplish these specialized tasks effectively, medieval town walls, following Roman tradition, consisted of three characteristic parts: wall, tower, and gate. One to two meters thick and frequently up to twenty meters high, the wall was an insurmountable obstacle to normal transit. Its dank shadow blanketed an area some fifty feet wide on either side. Every hundred feet or so the wall swelled out into a round or square tower. Broken by small openings, the towers provided the garrison within with a maximum field of cross fire on an attacking enemy. The critical points in the wall, however, were the gates. By definition weak points in the fabric, they were doubly protected by especially large and strong flanking towers. A river or other body of water bisecting a city created a similar breach in the walls and these points also received particular attention in the form of strong towers (Copenhagen, Fig. 5; Paris: Tour de Nesle, Fig. 7) or sometimes special water towers (Lucerne: Wasserturm, Fig. 9; Bremen: "Die Braut," Fig. 10). Sometimes the wall was built right across a body of water (Moscow, Fig. 11), at others a chain served the same purpose. More frequently the towns were walled off against the river bank (Mainz, Fig. 12; Avignon, Fig. 13; Vienna, Fig. 14; Magdeburg, Fig. 15) with special gates leading to landings or bridges.

GATES

In theory a town gate was a place through which one passed in and out of the city. In practice it was a place where one waited. If you arrived after the gate was closed, you waited for it to open. If it was open, you waited for the guards to inspect your goods and to collect the customary toll. The gate taxes were the major forms of income for the cities and it was right and proper that they be collected. A useful tool represents a capital investment, and no one should presume to take advantage of it without due payment.

At medieval town gates you waited. You waited, chatted, ate, drank, and slept. In a sense, it might be said that you waited so long that you no longer bothered to go in when the boom was finally lifted. Instead you settled down and built your own city in front of the walls. This is an exaggeration, of course, but basically it is true. You, or someone like you, decided that there was business to be done outside the gates where people were waiting to do business inside. So you built an inn along the road just outside the gate (Fig. 16). A bit risky, outside the protection of the walls, even in peacetime, to be sure; but then, the gate, its towers, and its guards were right across the way, and in times of war one could take refuge with friends inside town and hope for the best. Gradually a few artisans moved alongside to serve the travelers staying at the inn. A *faubourg* was born.

WALLS II

The walls of medieval cities were subject to an immutable law regarding their dimensions: they invariably followed the *smallest* possible perimeter! Every extension of the town diameter—every extra foot of wall—implied greater building costs, greater maintenance expenses, and a larger garrison for adequate defense. The attitude of the medieval man on the street regarding expenditure of public funds on enlarging the walls may be summed up with equal simplicity: as long as *his* house and *his* shop, *his* parish and *his* church were contained within the walls, then the wall was quite big enough. Let those who had been left without or whose quarters had grown up outside the walls (the *faubourgs*), pay for a bigger wall!

The story of medieval cities is of people trying to get *into* town, not out of it. Only in the city with its special legal status could you escape most of the trappings of a "down" but by no means entirely "out" feudalism. Only in the city were there the conditions and facilities for an existence based on the production and exchange of goods and services as opposed to the life of baron, soldier, and serf on the land outside. That, and that primarily, was what the medieval cities were for! The closer you could get to the center of the city which, with its crossing of roads, was the hub of the most intense urban activity, the better! Better also, it would seem, to be on the periphery but inside the walls than to be left outside altogether.

The problem of occupancy on or near the inner wall periphery, however, is related to the nature of the wall and the primary purpose of urban existence. One lived in the city in order to utilize it for the production and/or exchange of goods and services. While some of the products offered for sale could be manufactured away from the place of exchange (and most agricultural and other food products were, in fact, grown outside of the city), there was no inherent advantage in separating the place of production from the market. With the exception of food products, place of production and market were usually identical in the medieval town. But successful production and exchange of goods depended on adequate human traffic and the availability of secondary services which make for a good market, for example, good and direct access roads for cart delivery of raw materials, an ample supply of fresh water, a vicinity of notaries, town officials and churches, all necessary in the business of transactions by contract and oath and in the frequent litigations. Nearby schools of lower and higher learning also facilitated every kind of urban activity.

The man occupying a site near the wall, say, halfway between two gates with their arterial roads leading to the center, was in the worst possible position in town from every conceivable point of view. No one more fortunately placed had any reason to come to that location unless it was specifically to see *him*. This was a poor augury for business, unless one's product or service was indeed unique—an unlikely chance in a competitive world. The distance to the active center, moreover, was not only the longest, but unlikely to be a straight line route. More probably it would lead first to one of the radial routes connecting center and gates, then inward to the center. In both coming and going productive time was lost, and productive time in a non- or semi-mechanized economy spells success or failure.

These considerations explain a number of characteristics of the larger medieval cities. The over-all pattern of settlement within the walls was not, as might be supposed, one of concentric rings, but a starfish pattern. An inner cluster of a densely populated and, hence, wholly successful "central city" that was crisscrossed by the dense network of streets around its central market place or street, was surrounded by radiating arms of settlement along the arterial roads that led to the gates with a shading of secondary and parallel roads flanking these arteries (Liège, Fig. 17). The roughly triangular areas left between the main radial roads were frequently left unoccupied as late as the middle of the nineteenth century. Scattered houses stood here and there amid fields and vegetable gardens (Constance, Fig. 18, first circle; Florence, Figs. 19, 20), a kind of country within the city: the product of deficient viability.

THE POLITICS OF THE *FAUBOURGS*

At the same time that undesirable ground was left unsettled within the walls, the little settled clusters of economic activity along the roads just outside of the main town gates were mushrooming (Seville, Fig. 21; London, Fig. 22). If the gates and the temporary traffic block they represented had created the initial stimulus for this limited lodging and service industry outside the walls, growing traffic as well as saturation of the favorable business locations inside the walls soon gave the *faubourgs* a booming life of their own. As the intensity of economic activity within the walls increased, public market space on a new scale was required, and this could be found only outside the walls. The *faubourg* markets quickly turned into major satellite nuclei of economic life in competition with the older and usually smaller markets within the walls—markets, moreover, where the town gate and sales taxes could be avoided or, at least, more easily evaded. This consideration, together with their sheer growing economic power, must have been the political sledgehammer with which the *faubourgs* finally forced their inclusion inside an expanded ring of city walls (Breslau, Fig. 23). For whatever the limited advantages of a market in competition with the city, inclusion within the walls with all of the physical security, legal privileges, and economic opportunities that it implied—particularly if viability was enhanced by the demolition of the old inner wall ring—had greater attraction still. It was the expectation of this eventual inclusion within the magic circle of production and trade that had brought the hopeful future *franc bourgeois** to the foot of the walls in the first place. It was this eventuality that led him to prefer the potentially favorable location along the road outside the walls to a peripheral situation with limited prospects inside. It was for this occasion that he was waiting—and as often as not several generations continued to wait until that day came. Finally the economic pressure of the *faubourgs* and of growing populations within the cities could be denied no longer and the strategic

---

*As used in this volume, the term bourgeois has no political or class significance in the modern sense. It means anyone of humble or even aristocratic origins who lives in, works in, or uses the city.

risks and fiscal burdens of a new wall could no longer be resisted. Even so, the examples are numerous (Aachen, Figs. 24, 25; Strasbourg, Fig. 26; Geneva, Figs. 27, 28; Paris, Fig. 7; Barcelona, Fig. 29) where the power of the *faubourgs* was insufficient to force a simultaneous demolition of the old inner wall.

This turning point in the development of the greater of the medieval cities was reached in most parts of western Europe by the end of the thirteenth century. The succeeding centuries witnessed a gradual slowdown in the population explosion that had been the major historical phenomenon in western Europe in the twelfth and thirteenth centuries, and the growth process of the cities slowed down as well. Furthermore, the great polygonal outworks of sixteenth and seventeenth century fortifications, built for strategic defense against artillery attack, were of such massive, impenetrable scale and required such a wide open field of fire around them, that the formation of *faubourgs* farther out was discouraged (Strasbourg, Fig. 26; Augsburg, Fig. 30; Hamburg, Fig. 31). In spite of these obstacles, the new gates gradually provided the stimulus for yet another group of urban nuclei outside the walls and the cycle of mushrooming *faubourgs* began again (Vienna, Fig. 14).

BRIDGEHEADS

A bridge is a public street crossing a body of water, usually a river (Zürich, Fig. 32). Bodies of water, being traversable, were weak points, and medieval cities, as we have seen, were frequently walled off against them (Reims, Fig. 33; Trier, Fig. 34). By its nature a bridge just outside the town walls became a point of particular strategic importance. One or both of its ends were usually fortified with a gate tower (Heilbronn, Fig. 35; Bern, Fig. 36). In cases of particular vulnerability, a bridgehead castle was established to protect the approaches to the bridge itself (Avignon, Fig. 13; Paris, Fig. 7; Ulm, Fig. 37).

The pattern applying to gates in general is particularly relevant to fortified bridgeheads, since tolls for the upkeep of the bridge could be collected in addition to the usual gate taxes. Thus the bridgehead became a focal point for a *faubourg* (Reims, Fig. 33). These bridgehead *faubourgs*, however, were of more than usual concern to the city authorities since their capture could give an enemy a stranglehold on a key artery in and out of town; they were quickly fortified (Frankfurt-Sachsenhausen, Figs. 38, 39; Kassel-Unterneustadt, Fig. 40). Their isolated position, therefore, together with their strategic importance, gave these *faubourgs* political leverage and they frequently maintained a certain autonomy and separate identity well into the nineteenth century (London-Southwark, Fig. 41).

A main point of entrance on a river bank opposite a major city could develop into a *faubourg* even in the absence of a bridge. The crossing was accomplished by ferry boat. Cologne-Deutz, left without a bridge since Roman days and not incorporated into greater Cologne until the end of the nineteenth century when the present Hohenzollern Bridge was built, is an example (Cologne, Fig. 42).

PRIVATE SPACE—PUBLIC SPACE

I

There is a place, indeed there are usually several places in medieval cities which function as markets in one or in various commodities. Their names, Haymarket, Marché aux Poissons, Gänsemarkt, Campo de' Fiori, Mercato Vecchio, Nytorv, and so on, mark them for our attention. They are spots of colorful activity, of shouting and of movement, and many of them continue their useful function to this day. The existence of these specialized spaces dedicated to trade should not blind us to a basic fact: the *entire* medieval city was a market. Trade and production for trade went on in all parts of the city: in open spaces and closed spaces, public spaces and private spaces.

Space within the walls was limited. Two inherently different interests were competing for this space: private and public interests.

What the individual needed in the city was space for production, trade, and habitation—preferably in a favorable location for the first two, which are fundamental. The problem of economic survival being foremost in the rough-and-tumble of the developing medieval towns, habitation and its possible amenities took a decidedly second rank. In general, an individual's center of economic activity and his place of residence were identical. There was simply no economic justification for separating the two by any appreciable physical distance, regardless of their possible incompatibility.

Perhaps the most essential difference between public and private space within a city is their relative penetrability. Public space is, almost by definition, penetrable, i.e., accessible to all within relatively few limits. Private space, whether it be enclosed or open, is impenetrable. It cannot be used, crossed, or entered except by consent of the owner. But the production and exchange of goods and services, the basic purpose of the city, depends on buyer meeting seller, hence inevitably on free movement and interchange of goods and persons. Regardless, then, of the irresistible hunger for private space, it is countered by an immutable necessity: a city must have public space.

But traffic of goods and persons is not the only factor to be considered. There were, in addition, persons regularly within the city walls intent on legitimate business who owned no private space within the town in which to carry on their business. The most obvious representative of this species was the peasant, in town to market his produce and his livestock. Even if he should tarry overnight at an inn before returning to his village, in other words, hire himself a private space for temporary habitation—an unlikely event with cash scarce—he still needed a place to sell his goods. Obviously it had to be a public place. The peasant was not alone. There was also the occasional itinerant trader in rare goods, especially welcome in the smaller, less cosmopolitan towns. There were the traveling players. Buildings of public administration and various religious institutions also needed a certain amount of adjacent public space.

The resultant shape of the city, the character of its buildings, its streets, and its larger public spaces, is determined by the interaction of private and public interests. It is sometimes suggested that the medieval town "just grew," unplanned, if quaint and charming. Actually its formation was subject to definable patterns of economic, social, and political behavior.

II

In the instructions of the Spanish rulers to their *conquistadores* during the 16th century *(Laws of the Indies)*, a set pattern was laid down for the Spanish colonial towns to be established in the New World. Its characteristic features were a square, the *plaza mayor* dominating the center of town, surrounded by the chief administrative and religious buildings and a gridiron pattern of streets for residence. The idea derives from the standard plans of Roman and medieval colonial towns. By royal fiat a wide expanse of public space was created, regardless of the particular needs or prospects of the settlement involved. In some cases these spaces have fulfilled the expectations of the founders and have become the crowded focal point of lively public and commercial activity. In other cases royal intentions and the bitter realities of a poor location did not coincide and dusty squares parched by a merciless sun and shaken by periodic earthquakes are the squalid centers of hopeless poverty. Successes or failures, their potential was designed into them. The capital investment in basic buildings and landscaping either returned a profit or it did not. The design, in any event, was predetermined: a presumably rational solution for anticipated conditions, based on ancient precedent, and more or less immutable. Such urban planning was possible in a centrally administered national state with a wholly new scale of human and material resources at its disposal and with world-wide ambitions that demanded instant results. In such a situation risks could be taken, and a certain percentage of failure was discounted in advance.

I have introduced this example of Renaissance urban design as an illustration of how public space was *not* commonly created in medieval towns. The centralized political authority necessary to execute schematic plans of this kind was, by and large, wholly lacking, and material wealth, the capital ingredient necessary to create the tool a town represents, was in short supply (see Appendix I). In such circumstances no risks could be taken. Urban forms had to be suited to existing conditions—or rather, were shaped by these conditions.

The forces involved worked simultaneously in two directions: the elements requiring public space tended to push back the line of buildings, that is, private space, on all sides; private interests were constantly encroaching on public space up to the limit of their economic and political power. Since the medieval town was primarily a tool for the manipulation of economic forces, economic and political power were substantially identical, at least in theory. In practice some extraneous factors, still to be considered, artificially altered this ideal balance of urban forces.

III

Streets are the most basic and minimal units of public space in a city. But, as we have already noted, the need for viability in medieval towns was in direct conflict with the need for built-up private space. The resulting rule governing the width of streets may be stated simply: streets will be as *narrow* as they can be while allowing for transit of goods and persons. The tendency of buildings was to encroach on the adjoining streets (or other public space, e.g. the houses lining the bridges). The success of this encroachment depended on the relative political power of the builder involved. The irregular building lines of medieval towns (Fig. 43) testify to the varying status and power of the individuals involved.

The public records of medieval towns all over Europe abound with statutes governing the widths of streets, frontage lines which must not be exceeded, the minimum height at which a building projection was permissible, and so on. These control measures were more a symptom of the disease than its cure. Encroachment achieved its possible maximum when a house extended entirely across a street, leaving only an underpass of minimum height for viability. The Venetian *sottoportici* are surviving examples of this extreme. The abandoned inner walls, left standing for lack of incentive to demolish them, represent a form of marginal public space subject to encroachment and penetration. The poorer element squatted in the ruins. Richer bourgeois bought the towers and turned them into habitations. Other stretches of former wall composed one side of houses built up against them, through them, and over them.

IV

There are points in a town where the forces tending to expand public space will be concentrated and, by their very concentration, will widen the space around them. A prime example of such a point is the street immediately *inside* the town gates (Rome, Fig. 44). We have seen how the areas just *outside* the gates became focal points for urban expansion. The space just inside the gate has quite different aspects and uses. Its nature can best be understood by considering the position of a person with business to do in town, but without a private place to do it and who has just passed the gate. His period of waiting in front of the gate is finally over. He—let us say a peasant with produce to market—has at last reached his goal. He is *inside* the city, *in* the market. The way has been long. Presumably he started out from home before dawn. He has entered the town at the first opportunity after the gates have opened. He has arrived! He is not in town to see the sights; no special saint is being feted. It is an ordinary working day. What force, then, is there to draw him further into the city? His cart is heavy; why bother to move it further? Inside the gate is *in* and that is far enough. *There* he opens his stand and begins hawking his wares. Others join him. There is a market. It becomes traditional at that point and may even become specialized in a specific product. It turns into an economic force that gradually overwhelms flanking private interests. Little by little, in a gradual process of economic and political give-and-take, the street becomes wider near the gate, eventually assuming the form of a funnel with its wide end at the gate, gradually narrowing toward the center of town (Nuremberg, Kornmarkt, Fig. 45; Antwerp, Paardenmarkt, Fig. 53; Paris, Place Badoyer and Rue Saint-Antoine, Fig. 7; Munich, Neuhauserstrasse, Fig. 46; Piazza del Popolo before 19th century transformation, Fig, 44; Toledo, Fig. 47). The Italians call such a space a *largo*, a widening, suitably undefined geometrically.

V

All spaces, all streets, narrow or wide within the medieval town, were "markets" of some kind or degree. The larger spaces interrupting the dense network of narrow streets of medieval cities in the late phase in which we generally know them, bearing the name *"market," "torg," "plein,"* or some variation of the Latin *"platea,"* have a characteristic history and pattern of their own. In contrast to the Roman colonial towns (or their late medieval descendants referred to in Appendix I) where a central square was part and parcel of a predisposed plan, the early medieval linear or circular settlements from which most European cities developed in the eleventh century were too insignificant in scale or urban activity to include an organically defined "market place." Characteristically under these circumstances, the economic chicken of gradually intensified business activity preceded the urban egg of a built-up and enclosed *"platea."* The exceptions to this rule are centrally located, more or less rectangular market places surviving from ancient *capitolia* in former Roman towns like the Mercato Vecchio of Florence which flourished in the heart of the old city up to the time of its demolition late in the nineteenth century (Fig. 19).

More typically, these new concentrations of continuous or sporadic commercial activity grew up at the edge of the early settlements where ample open space was still available. Initially on unenclosed ground at the end of a street settlement (linear cluster) or just outside the gates of a walled *bourg* (circular or semicircular cluster), the physical size of these markets was limited only by their inherent economic potential. Around them developed the typical *faubourgs* we have already discussed, potent clusters of economic activity whose ultimate incorporation within an enlarged circle of town walls was an inevitable consequence. As the *platea* was gradually enclosed by the mushrooming *faubourg*, the typical conflict of expanding public and encroaching private space determined its ultimate form. The pressure of "public" activity, and thus the area of public space, decreased toward the periphery of the market area. The resulting shape of the market was a number of diverging "funnels," each diminishing in the direction of a street opening into the market.

The market place of Tübingen in Swabia (Figs. 48, 49) is a

classic example of this pattern. An urban settlement at the foot of the Burg Hohentübingen along the Neckar River is recorded as largely destroyed by fire in 1280 (Fig. 48). The surviving late medieval town is a product of reconstructions following repeated fires in the fifteenth and sixteenth centuries, when the place had a brief flowering as the residence of the Württemberg princes Graf Eberhard im Bart (d. 1496) and his son Graf Ulrich (d. 1550).

In its early period Tübingen consisted of two separate settlements (Fig. 48), the "Ammerstadt," a village of essentially rural character in the valley north of the Burg between the two branches of the Ammer River and a more typically urban settlement climbing up along the slopes of the Neckar River to the east below the Burg.[9] By the end of the eleventh century the periphery of the roughly elliptical "Neckarstadt" ran roughly from the site of the later Augustinian convent to the line Holzmarkt-Neckargasse in Weidle's somewhat hypothetical plan of the gradual growth of the town (Fig. 51), including the forerunner of the late Gothic Stiftskirche St. Georg (1470f.). From the crest of the slope along Kronengasse-Kirchgasse-Holzmarkt the terrain falls off towards the north into the Ammer valley. The establishment of the Augustinians at the western periphery of the "Neckarstadt" in 1262 and the foundation of the Franciscan cloister (the later *Collegium Illustre* and present Catholic Seminary) to the north in 1272 give an indication of the extent of the town in the thirteenth century and make it probable that at this point the two separate towns were gradually beginning to merge. This problem need not concern us. What is of interest is the location and form of the present main market place. In its early state the "Neckarstadt" had neither room nor need for a market place *intra muros*. It is, of course, hard to tell how far the surviving post-fifteenth-century buildings repeat the line of earlier structures, but it seems likely that a small market was originally formed at the western gate just inside the funnel-shaped widening at the head of the Münzgasse. Just outside the gate the *faubourg* houses lining the road leading up from the Neckar (Neckarhalde) enclosed a characteristic *faubourg largo* known as "Faules Eck" (Lazy Corner), a busy place in spite of its name. The main market of the "Neckarstadt," however, eventually moved just north of the walled town, spreading down the slope from the Kronengasse. As the growing town gradually engulfed the new market, extending northward to merge with the Ammerstadt in the valley below, the conflicting forces of public and private interest came into play. The almost straight line of buildings along the northern side of the market was prevented from intruding south into the public area by the sheer pressure of north-south traffic coming up from and going down into the Ammer valley along the Schmiedtorgasse, over the Ammer, crossing at the Krumme Brücke and filtering through the Marktgasse and the Hirschgasse, then eastward along Kirchgasse and Holzmarkt and down to the Neckar river through the Neckargasse (bottom right of plan). The houses flanking the market on its southeastern and south-western side, however, seem likely to be the result of gradual encroachment on the public space, leaving only a narrow opening into the market from the south.[10] This opening was still further reduced by the group of buildings jammed like a plug between the Wienergässle and the narrow flight of stairs running between the Kronengasse and the market place below. While the pressure of traffic between Kirchgasse and Hirschgasse led to the typical funnel-shaped widening at the southern end of the Hirschgasse, the pressure along the Marktgasse was so much less that there is not only no funnel at the corner of Marktgasse and Markt-platz, but the corner houses were actually able to encroach upon it, forming a bottleneck at the intersection.

The most striking example of encroachment of built-up on open space around the market is the Rathaus on its west side, built after 1433 (Fig. 49). We will come back to the question of public buildings, their scale and place within the medieval city. Suffice it to say here that no private individual within medieval towns ever had the power to intrude so radically into public space. Weidle suggests that the Haaggasse originally ran on a straight east-westerly path into the market. If this was the case—and it seems likely—then the southerly deviation of the Haaggasse at its eastern end and the almost complete blockage of its opening into the market place by the Rathaus represents an extreme example of the conflicting interaction of space and buildings in a medieval town.

Formations just outside earlier walls similar to the Tübingen market are common all over Europe (Avignon, "Le Change," Fig. 13; Vienna, Freyung, Fig. 14; Antwerp, Groote Markt, Fig. 52, and De Meir, Fig. 53; Florence, Piazza S. Maria Novella, Figs. 19, 20). Both the main produce market of Paris, Les Halles and its Left Bank counterpart, the Place Maubert (Fig. 7) have a form and history similar to the Tübingen market. When it was first established by Louis the Fat in 1137, the Les Halles market was outside the then existing *enceinte* of Paris, literally in the fields *(les champeaux)*. The earlier market in the Place de Grève on the river bank had become too confined by the encroachment of buildings, and the location had become isolated by the gradual crumbling of the old Roman bridge. With the new commercial center now focused on the St.-Jacques-la-Boucherie quarter at the head of the new bridge leading to the Rue Saint-Denis, main north-south artery of the growing commercial district, the new market found its place at the then periphery of town. Gradually engulfed by the expanding city during the twelfth century and eventually incorporated into the perimeter of King Philip Augustus' wall around 1200, its ultimate shape is the product of the funnels formed at the heads of the streets entering the market place from all directions.

But the form of a street, *largo*, or plaza was never permanently fixed in medieval cities except by artificial controls (as in the case of the Campo in Siena).[11] Infinitely expanding public space and eternally encroaching buildings remained in a fluid balance, ever changing as the contrasting forces changed in scale and importance.

INSTITUTIONS AND URBAN SCALE

PUBLIC BUILDINGS

The interaction of public and private space was the primary factor in determining the form of medieval cities. We have already observed that the irregular development of streets, *larghi*, and plazas was in part due to the relative and varying economic-political power of individuals (or groups of individuals) competing within the community for the acquisition of private space. The relative scale of open or built-up space acquired became a direct index of the strength of the competing interests.

Public interest gradually also demanded more than open spaces. The savagely conflicting forces within the rapidly growing cities required regulation and control. Such regulation, in turn, could be realized only through an orderly system of legislation and administration. The gradually evolving constitutions of the medieval cities vary considerably from place to place. Common to most of them is some form of town council with power to legislate and town officials with the power to administrate, adjudicate, and control. Common to all of them is the need for public buildings in which to carry out these functions.

The process of gradual enlargement of public power and the solution of its growing need for public space, open and enclosed, can be traced with particular clarity in Florence where some of the oldest and most significant public buildings of any medieval city survive. It is interesting to note that the early town councils held their sporadic meetings not in a structure specifically created for this purpose, but in private buildings, generally semi-fortified towers. The oldest major public building in the town, the Bargello (Fig. 54), was built in the years right after 1250 as a fortified residence for the *podestà* and his retinue. The function of the *podestà*, a knight of non-Florentine birth appointed for a year's term, was the administration of justice. The town had long outgrown the line of the wall enclosing the old Roman nucleus and had gotten its second *enceinte* around 1175 (Fig. 19).[12] This new outer belt of enclosed land was still far from filled up in 1250, but there was simply no space for a public building the size of the new Palazzo del Podestà within the older inner core of town. It found its place on the outer side of the street marking the line of the former first wall. Both the new scale of this building and the new scale of the enlarged

36

perimeter are symptoms of a gradual rearrangement of urban forces in the rapidly rising city.

When the great symbol of Florentine power, the Palazzo della Signoria, was finally built around 1300 after a half century of internecine conflict between Guelfs and Ghibellines over the nature of the town constitution, public power was sufficient to force a place for both this gigantic building and its adjoining open *piazza* within the limits of the inner city; not at its heart, however, but at the extreme southeastern corner of the old town (Fig. 19). This encroachment of public on private space within the oldest part of the city, furthermore, was possible only through confiscation of the extensive property of the exiled Uberti clan.

The guilds formed the effective political and economic organization of the bourgeois, but bourgeois conservatism kept the guild residences small and unpretentious in scale during the centuries of greatest guild power.[13] Typically they had a guild office and archives for ordinary administration on the lower floor and a *sala magna* (usually much more modest in scale than the grandiloquent name implies) for the meetings of the guild consuls on the upper floor. The great guild halls of the Italian, German, and Flemish cities are a product of later centuries (15th–16th) when the guilds were in gradual process of decline: Parkinson's Law in action during the waning middle ages!

Public buildings may be a public necessity, but in contrast to most public spaces, they are not always fully accessible or penetrable. In this sense they tend to form an "institutional block" within the urban framework, whose particular characteristic is that one has to walk around it. Depending on the scale of the building involved, such a block can become a tumor in the urban fabric, one which discourages normal urban activity in its immediate vicinity. Le Stinche, the great square prison block built on expropriated Uberti land at the edge of Florence around 1300 is a classic example. It is interesting to note how this disadvantage can be overcome by providing for adequate penetrability. The Florentine cathedral, a decidedly "public" building and as gigantic a block of masonry as was ever inserted into an existing urban environment (Fig. 19), presented no problems whatever in this respect, by the simple expedient of providing two doors on either side of its gigantic nave (Fig. 55). At present only one of these side doors (the Porta della Canonica) is open to the public, and the building stands as a massive block between the northern and southern portions of the late medieval city.

Such, however, was not the case originally. With all four doors open, pedestrian traffic (and perhaps even an occasional cart and mule) could cross easily from the streets to either side of the cathedral: the great structure was not a block, but a place of lively cross traffic in which the passerby could, perhaps, find a moment of repose and devotion on his busy way. Great buildings serve the city best when they form an easily penetrable part—and not a block in the way—of the city's functioning apparatus!

THE CATHEDRALS

This hint of the urban problems presented by the great cathedrals of the medieval cities also provides an indication of the nature of their transformation from the twelfth century on. The bishoprics of the early medieval period generally had their origins in late antiquity. With some prominent exceptions in the lands east of the Rhine and north of the Danube, the old bishop's churches generally stood in towns of antique origins. Typically they were located at the periphery of the antique towns (Pisa, Rome) or just outside (Vienna, Fig. 14; Florence, Fig. 19) where the Christian population was concentrated (see discussion of Dura-Europos, p. 13 above). In the feudal period, with the increasing power of the bishops, cathedrals frequently underwent a first enlargement. With the revival of the cities, the power of the bishops diminished while the power of the bourgeois increased. This bourgeois power expressed itself primarily in the building of rings of family or guild chapels around the cathedrals, a process of growth and transformation which may be considered the liturgical core of Gothic architecture.[14] In a final analysis "Gothic architecture" and "medieval city architecture" become synonymous. Gothic art and architecture are the expression of the revival of the cities during the twelfth and thirteenth centuries. The bishop's cathedral became the symbol, the pride, and the possession of the cities.

THE PARISHES

If the cathedral was the pride of the bourgeois, his parish church was a daily necessity. His birth, life, and death—his very identity—were inextricably bound up in it. The parish defined the limits of his legal existence and often his economic possibilities as well. The legality of contracts depended on sworn witnesses, and deeds were frequently written in the churches where oaths could be taken on the sacred relics. The parish

38

church became the obvious burial place of the leading families. The adjoining cemeteries served the poor. Parish market and parish church logically adjoined each other as the mercantile, legal and religious center of the parish unit within the urban fabric (Stettin, Fig. 56). The parish boundaries generally had their origins in feudal land ownership. The increasing power and dynamism of the cities gradually transformed the urban parishes into larger and more manageable units centering around the growing quarters of the expanding cities.[15]

THE MENDICANT ORDERS

Diocese and parish were the ancient units of urban organization, gradually penetrated and transformed by the rising bourgeois. But the growth of the cities presented new social problems of a kind unknown in the feudal period. The root of the problem lay in the gradual dissolution of the feudal order itself. While the merchant found his place and his political organization within the guilds, the untrained and illiterate peasant who became the urban worker formed a proletariat of the starving and the hopeless which presented social, political, and religious problems of unprecedented proportions. The expression of this hopelessness was, typically, religious heresy, a questioning of the underlying bases of the existing society. The late medieval answer to this challenge was the mendicant orders.[16]

While the Cistercians had approached the problems of declining feudalism with a program of pioneering in virgin lands, the mendicants were urban-oriented from their inception. Their mission was twofold: to aid the afflicted and to purge the heretic. Since afflicted and heretic were to be found not infrequently in the same skin, the task of the mendicants was a delicate one. It could be accomplished only by men prepared to live like the afflicted and among them. But this mass of unfortunates was figuratively and literally on the periphery of medieval urban society (as the Early Christians had been on the edge of the late antique milieu). The place, shape, and scale of the mendicant convents and churches were determined by this reality.

When the friars of St. Francis, St. Dominic, and of the other mendicant orders arrived in the medieval cities seething with the social, political, and religious ferment of a society in rapid evolution, the space within the old urban cores was already filled with the cathedral, the parish churches, and the towers and houses of the urban nobility and the bourgeois patricians. The ancient abbeys of the Benedictines were on or near the edge of the old towns, frequently just outside (Paris, St.-Germain-des-Prés, Fig. 7). There was no room left in the center for the mendicants and it would have been pointless for them to settle there in any case. The people they sought and who needed them were on the periphery or in the *faubourgs* outside the walls. The economics of real estate values and simple practicality dictated the sites the mendicants acquired (usually as a pious gift from wealthy patricians). Paris and Florence are classic examples of this pattern.

In Paris the Left Bank of the city had remained a semi-urban expanse of vineyards even after its enclosure within the wall of Philip Augustus around 1200 (Fig. 7). While the main arteries (e.g., the Rue Saint-Jacques) were lined by houses, the less desirable areas near the walls remained unsettled. Here the Dominicans (Jacobins) and the Franciscans (Cordeliers) found their place in the early decades of the thirteenth century. The Servites settled along the wall on the Right Bank at the very edge of the commercial center. The Carmelites remained outside the walls in the Faubourg Saint-Paul. Their place was later taken by the Celestines.

When the monks arrived in Florence in those years, the area within the second wall, built around 1175, was nearly filled. What little was left was, in any case, insufficient to contain the great barnlike churches that followed the earliest foundations of the mendicants. Huge halls were what was needed to preach faith and orthodoxy to an urban population numerically unprecedented since Early Christian days.[17] All of the great mendicant order churches in Florence, S. Maria Novella (Dominicans), S. Croce (Franciscans), SS. Annunziata (Servites), Ognissanti (Osservanti), S. Spirito (Augustinians), and the Carmine (Carmelites) were outside the city walls at the time of their establishment (Fig. 19, 20).[18] The large public spaces that remain in front of these churches and characterize them (Florence: Piazza S. Croce, Piazza S. Maria Novella, Piazza del Carmine) are the surviving *faubourg* markets outside the gates of the old wall rings.

It may be said that the stability that the mendicant convents brought to the turbulent *faubourgs* contributed to that growing political and economic power which eventually made the inclusion of the *faubourgs* within the later wall a matter of interest not only to the residents of the *faubourgs*, but to the city as a whole.

40

HOSPICES AND HOSPITALS

Cities have problems. The starving need food and temporary shelter; the sick and dying need hospitals; the dead, cemeteries. In a sense all of this was related to the problem of efficient waste elimination. Garbage and night soil were carted to dumps outside the walls. Street dirt and manure were washed away by rain, and the rivers were more important as open sewers than as traffic arteries. Growing populations, poor sanitation, vermin, and impure water led to recurring epidemics. In the fourteenth century this problem reached disastrous proportions culminating in the Black Death (1348–1349). Hospices (pious foundations) spread around the cities—usually near the gates—and took in pilgrims and wandering beggars, feeding and housing them for nothing. The hospitals, separate long dormitory halls for men and women flanking a courtyard and sometimes with a loggia facing the street, were built by pious donors on their own property or on cheap land near or outside the walls. Volunteer nurses organized in semi-religious orders cared for the sick and dying. Service was free. The costs were covered by the income from gifts and legacies.

UNIVERSITIES

Learning in the Middle Ages was a digest of ancient law, philosophy, literature, and science with an admixture of Christian theology. In the feudal period the Benedictines nourished a restricted circle of monastic scholars and clerks. The cities required a much greater supply of trained jurists, notaries and scribes for the administration of public and private business. The great universities founded in Paris, Padua and Bologna, and on a smaller scale elsewhere from the middle of the thirteenth century on, filled this need. Their sites, usually on donated land, followed the pattern of the mendicant convents and the hospitals. In Paris, for example, the numerous independent colleges comprising the university of scholars found their place on the less developed southern side of town among the foundations of the mendicant friars, and the Left Bank became known simply as the University. The king's palace and the bishop's cathedral were on the Ile de la Cité. The merchants' city was on the Right Bank. The students relaxed, played and fought on the *Prés aux clercs* (Scholars' Field) outside the Porte de Bussy in the shadow of the walls of the Merovingian abbey of Saint-Germain (around which they gather to this day) (Fig. 7).

CITY AND ANTI-CITY

THE PRINCES AND THE TOWNS

The medieval city was the tool of the merchant, but the land on which it was built and the country around it was not his. The feudal system of land ownership and legal privilege which antedated the growth of the medieval towns sturdily outlived their gradual evolution and decline, not to expire finally until the age of Napoleon. Since the wealth and power of the magnates was based on land ownership acquired by military prowess, these men were by nature anti-urban. But they owned the land, and their military power was a factor with which the bourgeois had to live, unless he was strong enough to defeat it—and this was generally not the case.

We have discussed the medieval city in its ideal form: the free and independent city republic run by and for the bourgeois and dominating a wide area of agricultural land around it. But this ideal was attained by only a few of the most powerful cities in Italy and in the North, and usually only after bloody struggles against the landed nobility (Guelf-Ghibelline wars in Italy). In the North, particularly in Central Europe, the secular and ecclesiastical barons and princes and their fortified residences remained a significant and characteristic part of the medieval cities.[19]

The interests of the princes and the bourgeois were in contradiction even when this did not involve open conflict. The feudal magnates were neither artisans nor merchants. They were subject to a different law than the bourgeois. Thus their existence in and value to the city was necessarily a marginal one. Sooner or later the parties settled down to a more or less mutually beneficial coexistence, but the fundamental contradictions remained.

As a voracious parasite, taking his share of the gate and market taxes in return for "protection," there was no proper place for the feudal magnate in town. Characteristically *Burg* and town formed separate entities. The fortress on its rocky height dominated the town and its approaches. The town nestled below in its shadow, perpetually reminded of its physical dependence (Avignon, Fig. 13; Salzburg, Fig. 57; Tübingen, Fig. 50; Heidelberg, Fig. 58). In Paris and Berlin the *seigneur* sat on an island, separate and fortified against the merchants' city. But the cities razed the magnates' towers and liquidated the nobles the moment they were powerful enough to do so (e.g., in

Florence and Siena at the end of the thirteenth century).

When the princes moved into town, the nature of their primarily military function made it logical that they should establish their residence on or in immediate proximity to the wall. As we have already noted, in the case of the Bargello in Florence (which was the seat of a formally invited non-Florentine aristocratic "protector of the peace") there was simply no room *in* town for a fortified aristocratic residence. It *had* to be on the edge (Nancy, Fig. 59). Invited or self-imposed, the magnates followed the same pattern in numerous medieval cities. It is particularly clear in Munich (Fig. 46) where the princely residence moved outward with the successive wall circles. The Alter Hof, residence of the thirteenth and fourteenth century Wittelsbacher princes, was on the vulnerable eastern flank of the inner wall. The Neue Residenz of the Renaissance dukes resumed the same position on the expanded wall. The ducal gardens were outside the walls (Hofgarten). The fortress of the Louvre which became the residence of the kings of France in the 16th century (Fig. 7) and the Hofburg in Vienna (Fig. 14) are in the same pattern, as were Stettin (Fig. 56) and Stuttgart (Fig. 60). As the power of the princes and the new urban nobility of the Renaissance—increasingly based on the resources of the nation as a whole—grew and the independence of the cities diminished from the fourteenth century onward, the residences of princes and nobility with their gardens and dependencies increased in magnitude and splendor as well, gradually becoming immense cancerous blocks to the organic existence and growth of the cities. But by then the cities were no longer within the control of the bourgeois—a situation which did not change until the French Revolution.

DECLINE

The political ideal and the ideal physical form of the free medieval cities were based on the general notion that all those who used the city were equal—equally citizens, that is. But from the very beginnings in the eleventh century it was perfectly clear that some of the bourgeois were "more equal" than others; both the political constitutions and the unending intramural struggles that marked the history of the medieval cities were the product of this reality. Certain of the trades and their guild organizations—wholesale export-import of textile goods and banking, for example—dominated the urban economies, while the minor trade guilds played a subordinate role economically and politically. The manual workers in the larger industries (textile weaving and dyeing) were frequently not allowed to form trade organizations at all and were totally disenfranchised (as in Florence).

By the middle of the fourteenth century there were at least three major strata of bourgeois within the urban walls: a small upper class oligarchy of wealthy merchants and an urban nobility living on income from properties and investments; a middle class of small traders and artisans; and a large but economically and politically weak lower class of laborers living on the margin of urban society. We have already discussed the social and political problems created by this urban proletariat. But the upper class gave the characteristic imprint to the late medieval city in evolution.

The dynamism of the upper class in the relatively few cities that remained free of domination by feudal lords, or by the upstart *condottieri* who appeared with increasing frequency in the Italian towns in the fourteenth century, lay in the fact that it was open to *novi homines*—except in Venice where the ranks of the urban patriciate were officially closed late in the thirteenth century. But the ruthless business competition of the period led inevitably to ever smaller and more powerful merchant oligarchies, eventually dominated by one or a few potent individuals (Medici, Fugger). This development had a decisive influence on the shape and function of medieval cities in their late phase.[20]

The most obvious and the most significant architectural symptom of this process is a change in the scale of upper class houses. From the last quarter of the fourteenth century on, the leading merchants and the urban nobility began building town palaces of much greater size. The chief problem, soluble through preponderant economic and political power, was the acquisition of adequate building plots in the old cities that were crowded with the narrow houses of an earlier era.

By the middle of the fifteenth century the town house of the oligarchs had changed not only in scale but also in function and appearance. The business houses and banking tables of the leading merchants were naturally in the very core of the old cities around the central markets—and like all bourgeois they had traditionally lived in and over their shops. But not even the most powerful patricians could seriously consider building their large new houses on these old sites. Not only could they not economically assemble adequate building sites in the crowded old center: they would have destroyed the market—the productive heart of the city—in the process. As a result the new palaces grew up in the less active periphery.

The inevitable by-product of this development was that for the first time in the history of the medieval cities, residence and place of business became separated. It is no coincidence that the first signs of the process appeared in Florence, the leader of the Early Renaissance cities. The Medici had their bank and their residences in the very heart of the old city, near the Mercato Nuovo (Figs. 19, 20). Giovanni d'Averardo de' Medici, the founder of the family fortune and conservative to the end, never thought of moving out of his old house in town. With his son, Cosimo, the old order changed. In the 1430's he began buying up sites around a few houses he owned in the Via Larga away from the center along the line of the former second town wall. Around 1450 the great house built by Michelozzo was finished, among the first and certainly the most significant of the new Renaissance town palaces *all' antico*.[21] Cosimo tended more and more to receive clients in the loggia in the corner of his new house—but the bank remained in its old place. The break had been made. Residence and shop, production and consumption became separate. The bourgeois became a commuter. The move to the suburbs that marks the following centuries had begun: it was the beginning of the end of the medieval cities.

ILLUSTRATIONS

All illustrations are by Mattheus or Caspar Merian unless otherwise specified. All the views and plans by Merian or Braun and Hogenberg are of the date of the publication in which they seem first to have appeared. For precise sources see pp. 118 and 127.

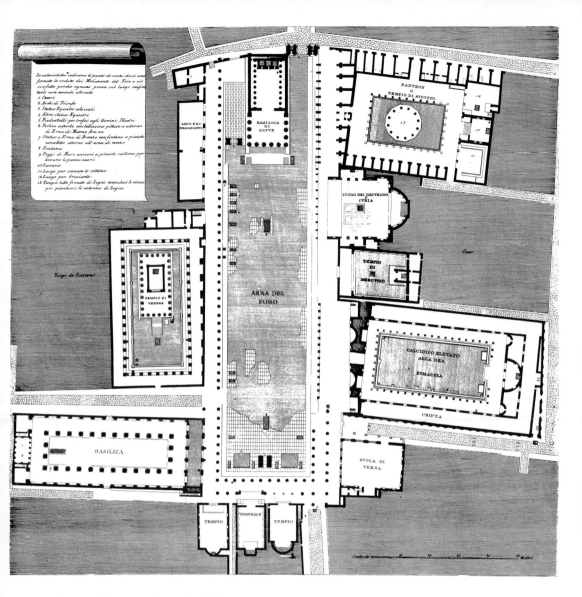

1. Pompeii, Forum (Rossini), 1830.

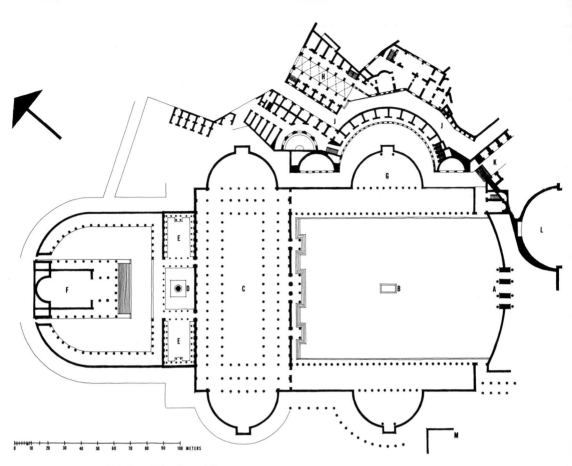

2. Rome, Forum of Trajan (MacDonald).

3. Dura-Europos, City Plan (Goodenough).

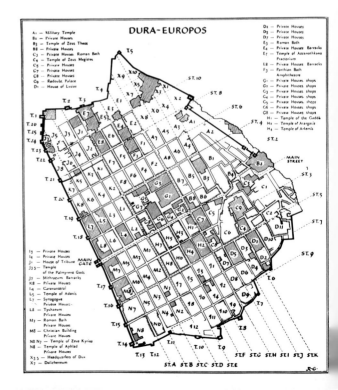

DURA-EUROPOS

A1 — Military Temple
B1 — Private Houses
B3 — Temple of Zeus Theos
B8 — Private Houses
C3 — Private Houses, Roman Bath
C4 — Temple of Zeus Megistos
C5 — Private Houses
C7 — Private Houses
C8 — Private Houses
C9 — Redoubt Palace
D1 — House of Lysias

D2 — Private Houses
D5 — Private Houses
D7 — Private Houses
E3 — Roman Bath
E4 — Private Houses, Barracks
E7 — Temple of Azzanathkona
Praetorium
L8 — Private Houses, Barracks
F3 — Parthian Bath
Amphitheatre
G1 — Private Houses, shops
G2 — Private Houses, shops
G3 — Private Houses, shops
G4 — Private Houses, shops
G5 — Private Houses, shops
G6 — Private Houses, shops
G8 — Private Houses, shops
H1 — Temple of the Gaddé
H2 — Temple of Atargatis
H4 — Temple of Artemis

I3 — Private Houses
I4 — Private Houses
J1 — House of Tribune
J3 — Temple
of the Palmyrene Gods
J7 — Mithraeum, Barracks
K8 — Private Houses
L4 — Caravanserai
L5 — Temple of Adonis
L7 — Synagogue
Private Houses
L8 — Tychaeum
Private Houses
M7 — Roman Bath
M8 — Christian Building
Private Houses
N7 — Temple of Zeus Kyrios
N8 — Temple of Aphlad
Private Houses
X3 — Headquarters of Dux
X7 — Dolicheneum

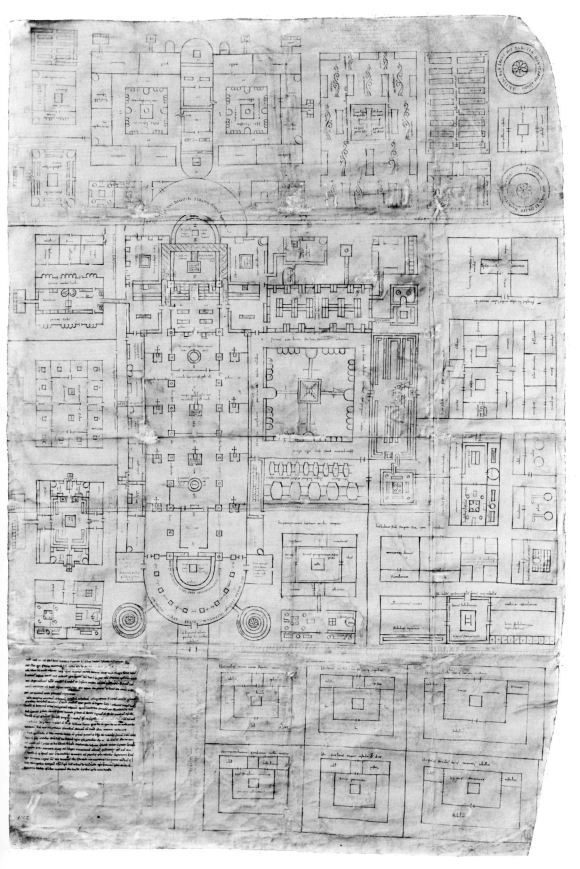

4. Monastery Plan of St. Gall, early 9th century.

5. Copenhagen, a Merian print with remarkably detailed topographical analysis, c. 1630—1640.

6. The town of Coblenz under attack, 1632.

7. Paris, "Trois Personnages," Plan, 1538.

1. Faubourg Saint Marceau
2. Les Halles (market place)
3. Île de la Cité
4. The Louvre
5. Place Badoyer

PARIS pour vray est la maiſõ royalle, Inde en eſtude, & en poetes Romme, Fecunde en vin, doulce en ſes Citoyẽs
Du dieu Phœbus en ſplendeur radiale Athenes lors en māit tresſcauāt homme, Fertile en bled, & en maintz daultres
Ceſt Gyrrhea pleine de bons eſpritz, Rozier mondain, baulme du firmament, ſbiens.
Tresuigoureux, faiſans diuers eſcriptz, Vniuerſel, de Sidon lomment,
Ceſt Chryſea en metaulx habondante Tres habondante en viures et breuuaiges,
Grece de pris en liures floriſſante Riche en beaulx champs & fluuieux riuaiges

Cum Priuilegio

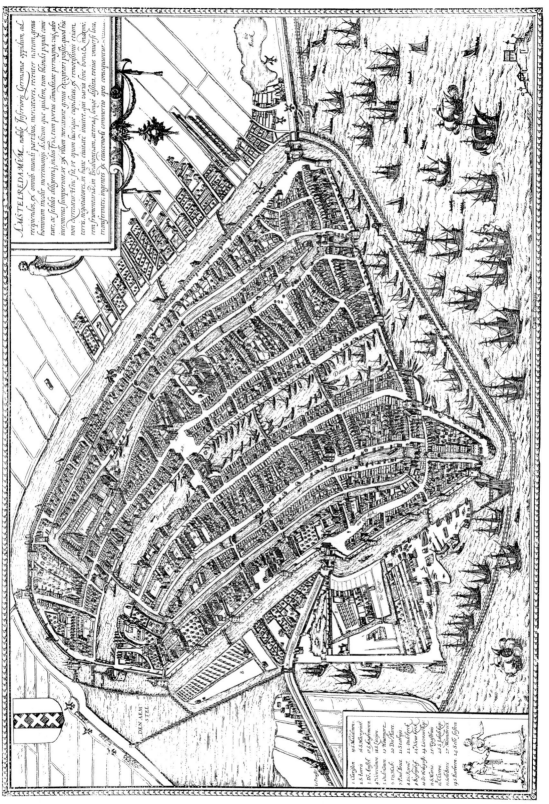

8. Amsterdam (Braun and Hogenberg), 1574.

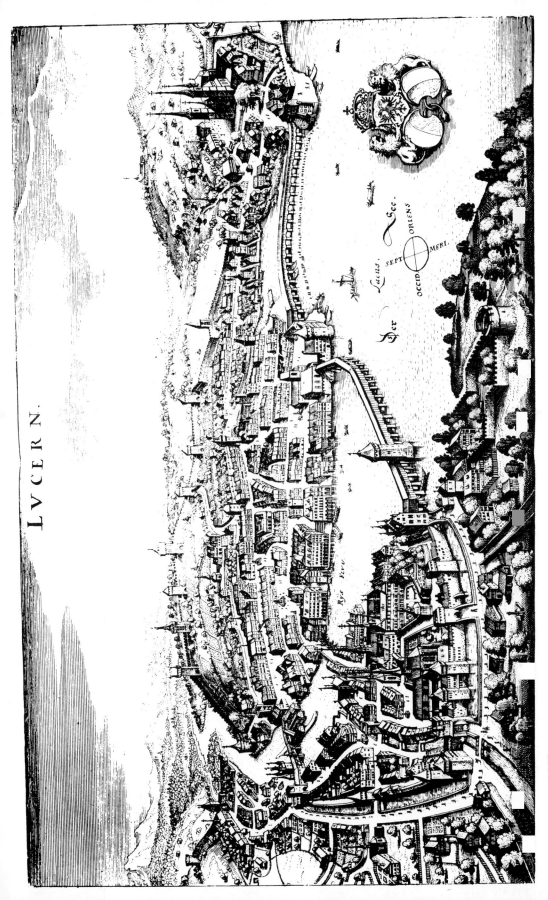

9. Lucerne, 1642.

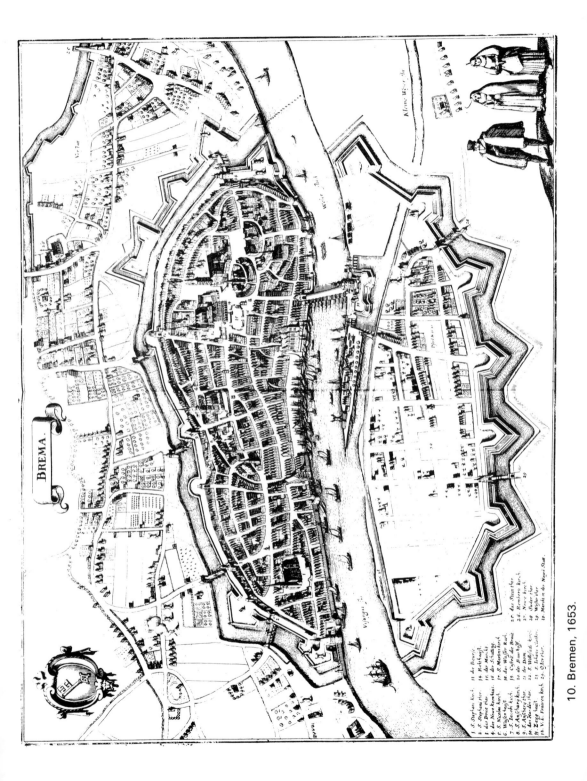

BREMA.

1. S. Stephan. kirck
2. S. Stephan. thor
3. der Daue thor
4. das Neue Baruhaus
5. S. Nicolai. kirck
6. S. Martens. kirck
7. Rathaus
8. S. Jacobs kirck
9. S. Ansgary. kirck
10. das Ansgary. thor
11. das Herden. thor
12. Zeug haus
13. U. L. Frauen. kirck

14. das Brauic
15. Rathaus
16. der Marckt
17. der S. ding
18. S. Mantenkirch
19. S. Mantenkirch
20. der Wasser Kirch
21. Capell des Dom
22. der Dom. hof
23. der Dom
24. S. Wilhade. kirck
25. S. Johan. closter
26. S. Oster. thor

27. der Stein. thor
28. Remberte. kirck
29. Neue kirck
30. Neue thor
31. Stader thor
32. Wester. thor
33. Merckt in der Neue. Stat

10. Bremen, 1653.

A. Krucskoug-gorod.
B. Ktay-gorod Vrbs media.
C. Tzargorod Vrbs exterior.
D. Skorodom, Vrbs exterior.
E. Strelerka sloboda. vel Vicus militaris.
J. Curia.
2. Patriarcheion.
3. Templ. D. Michaelis.
Sepret. sepultura.
4. Podium Ecclesiastico rum in supplicationibus.
Imperat. destinatum.
5. Taberna mercatoria.
6. Tabernake Vrbanæ.
7. Kglesii æromentarij.
8. Forum equarium.
9. Balneæ publicæ.
10. Forum lignarium.
11. Viridarium dmperat.
12. Lapis.

11. Moscow, 1646.

12. Mainz, 1646.

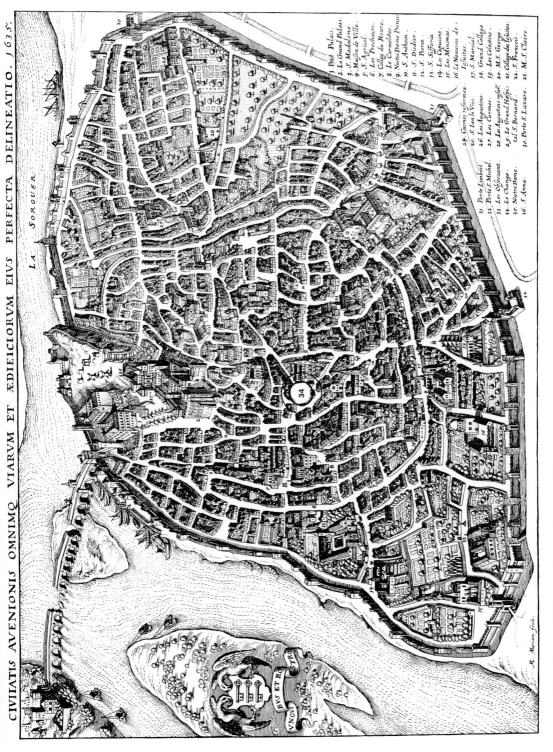

13. Avignon, 1635. Le Change is at no. 34.

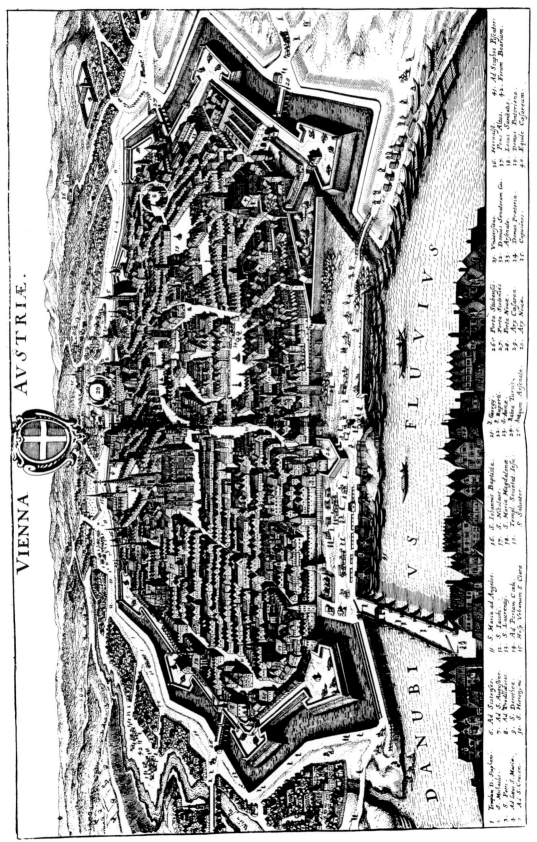

14. Vienna, 1677. The Freyung is open space to the left of no. 6; the Hofburg is at no. 29.

15. Magdeburg, 1645.

16. H. Pleydenwurff, Crucifixion, c. 1475-1500.

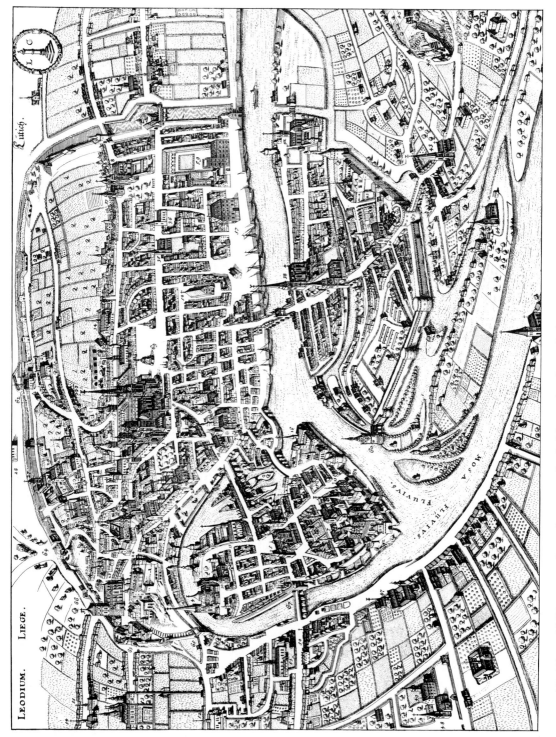

17. Liège, 1647, a complicated topography held together by radiating arteries.

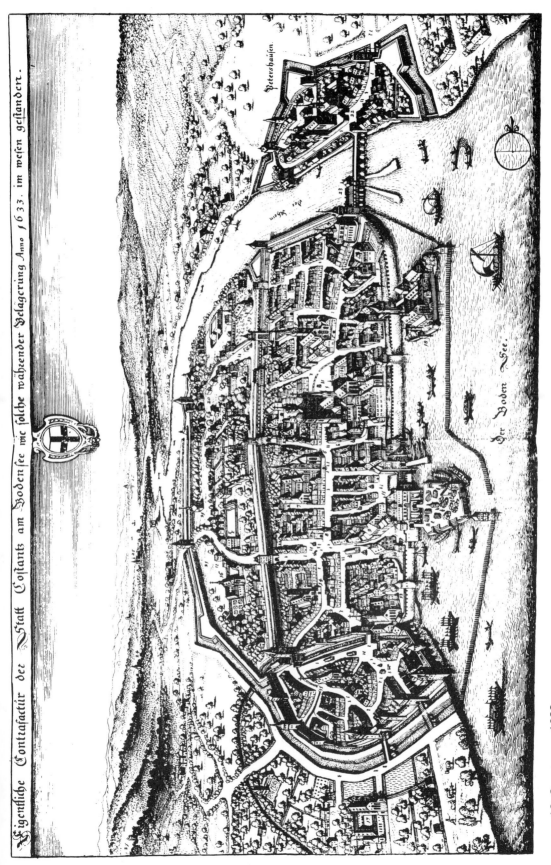

18. Constance, 1633.

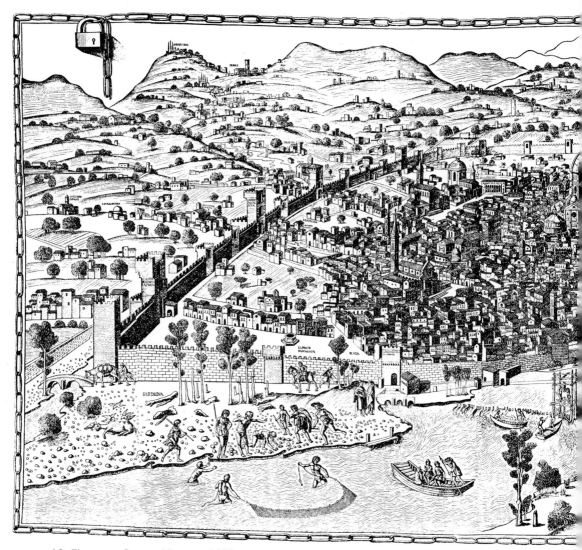

19. Florence, Catena View, c. 1470.

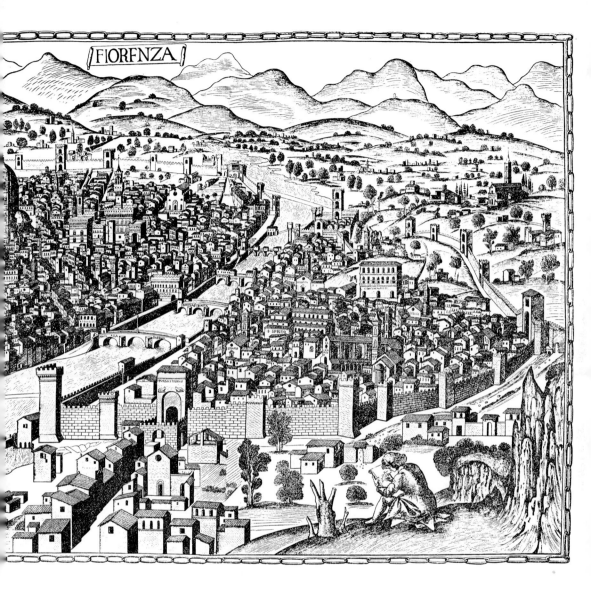

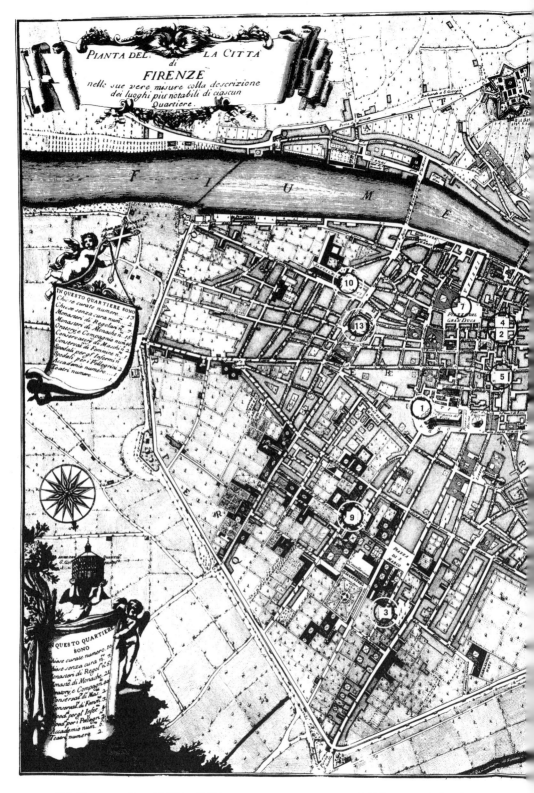

20. Florence, Zocchi Plan, 1754.

1. Il Duomo and the piazza
2. Former site of the Medici Bank
3. Via Larga
4. Mercato Nuovo

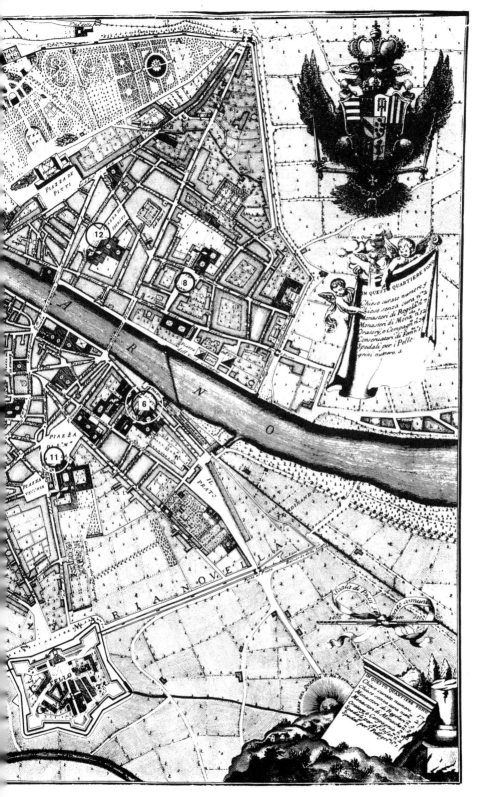

5. Mercato Vecchio
6. Ognissanti and the piazza
7. Palazzo della Signoria and the piazza
8. Piazza del Carmine

9. SS. Annunziata and the piazza
10. S. Croce and the piazza
11. S. Maria Novella and the piazza
12. S. Spirito and the piazza
13. Le Stinche

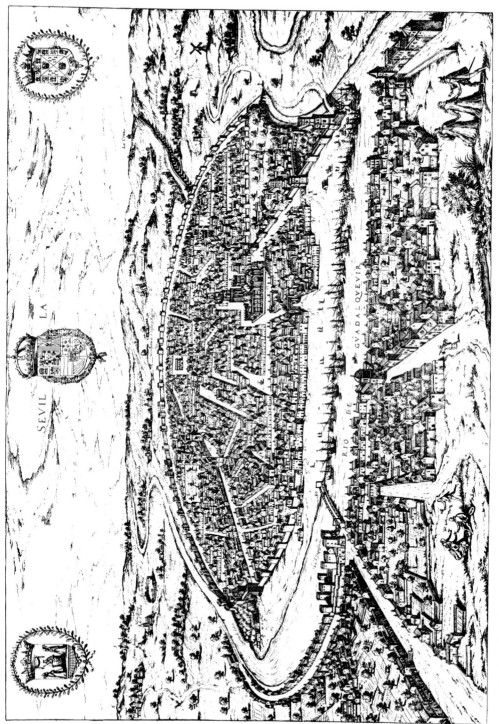

21. Seville (Braun and Hogenberg). c. 1574.

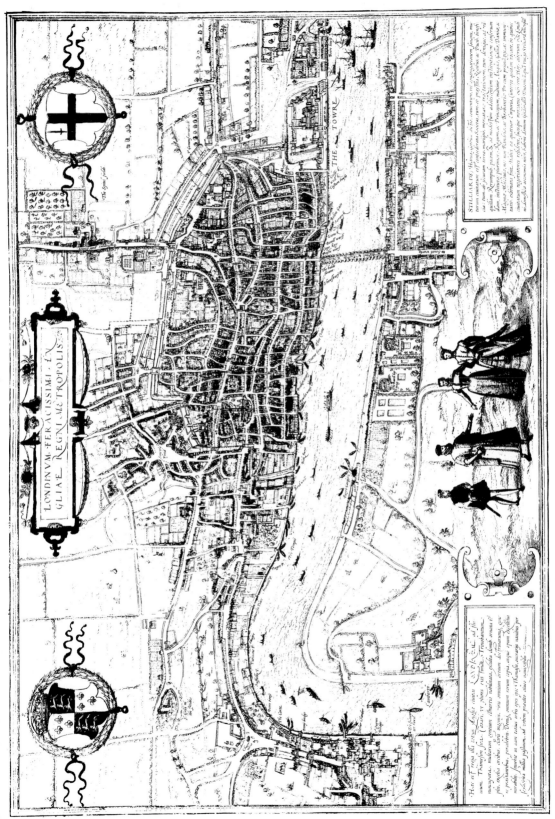

22. London (Braun and Hogenberg), c. 1574.

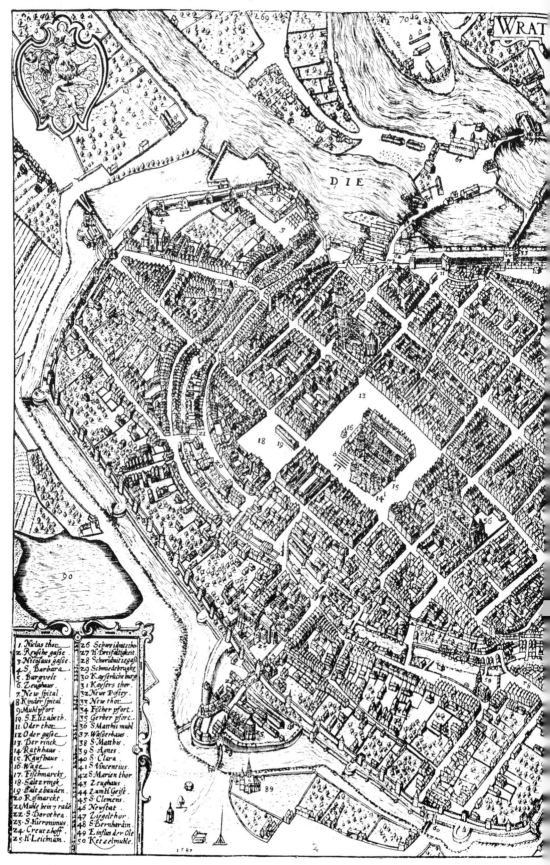

WRAT

DIE

1. Niclas thor
2. Reusche gasse
3. Nicolaus gasse
4. S. Barbara
5. Burgvelt
6. Zeughaus
7. New spital
8. Kinder spital
9. Muhl pfort
10. S. Elizabeth
11. Oder thor
12. Oder gasse
13. Der rinck
14. Rathhaus
15. Kaufhaus
16. Wage
17. Fischmarckt
18. Saltz ringk
19. Saltz bauden
20. Rosmarckt
21. Muhle bein 7 radt
22. S. Dorothea
23. S. Hieronimus
24. Creutz hoff
25. H. Leichnam

26. Schweidnitz tho
27. H. Dreifaltigkeit
28. Schweidnitz gass
29. Schmiedebrucke
30. Kayserliche burg
31. Kaysers thor
32. Newe Postey
33. New thor
34. Fischer pfort
35. Gerber pfort
36. S. Matthis muhl
37. Wasserhaus
38. S. Matthis
39. S. Agnes
40. S. Clara
41. S. Vincentius
42. S. Marien thor
43. Zeughaus
44. Zum H. Geist
45. S. Clemens
46. Newstat
47. Ziegel thor
48. S. Bernhardin
49. Einflus der Ole
50. Ketzelmuhle

23. Breslau (Braun and Hogenberg), 1590.

LAVIA·

ODER

FLVV.

51 S. Albricht.
52 Albrichts gasse.
53 S. Catharina.
54 Newmarckt.
55 Heringbauden.
56 S. Maria Magdale.
57 Ohsche thor.
58 Ohsche gasse.
59 S. Christophorus.
60 Taschenthor.
61 Vor der mühlen.
62 Wasserhaus.
63 Mittelmühle.
64 Maltzmühle.
65 Schleiff mühle.
66 Brettmühle.
67 Hinter mühle.
68 Papyr mühle.
69 Burger werder.
70 Schieswerder.
71 Walckmühle.

72 Elbing.
73 Eilf 1000 Jungfraw
74 S. Claren mühle.
75 H. Leichnams mühl.
76 S. Marien mühle.
78 S. Anna.
79 der Sant.
80 der Thun.
81 S. Petri und Pauli.
82 S. Martinus.
83 die Burgk.
84 H. Creutz.
85 S. Ioannes.
86 Bischof's hoff.
87 Ziegelscheune.
88 vor S. Mauritio.
89 New begrebnus.
90 Meyseteich.
91 Saltzhaus.
77 S. Maria.

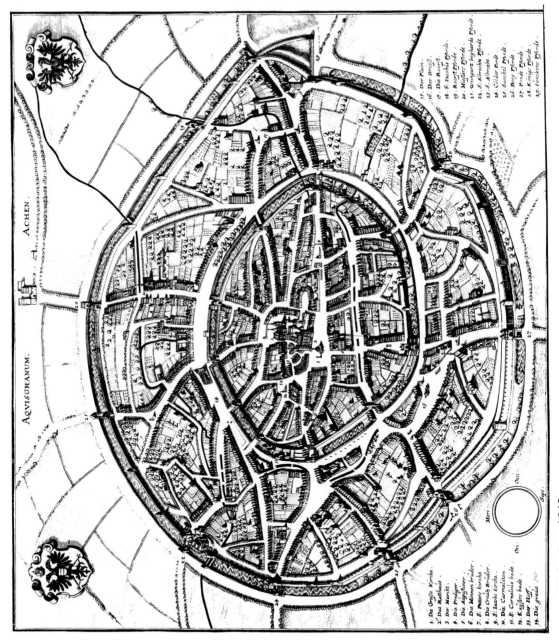

24. Aachen, 1649.

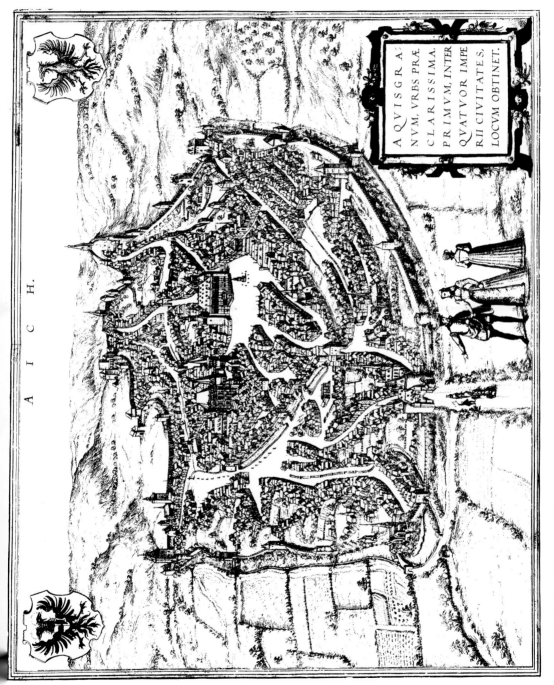

AQVISGRA
NVM, VRBS PRÆ
CLARISSIMA.
PRIMVM, INTER
QVATVOR IMPE
RII CIVITATES,
LOCVM OBTINET.

25. Aachen (Braun and Hogenberg), 1574.

ARGENTINA.

Straßburg.

1. Die Rhein brück.
2. S. Clair in Vndis.
3. New thor.
4. S. Wilhelm.
5. S. Staffan.
6. S. Catharina.
7. Gulden thurn.
8. Zun Rewern.
9. Iung S. Peter.
10. Münster.
11. Zeughauß.
12. Die Pfalz.
13. Prediger Closter.
14. Iung S. Peter.
15. Pfenning thurn.
16. Barfüffer Closter.
17. S. Niclaus.
18. Spital thor.
19. Spital.
20. Aller Heiligen.
21. Frauen bruder.
22. S. Thoman.
23. Alt S. Peter.
24. S. Marcur.
25. Im Bruch.
26. Steinstraßer thor.
27. S. Johann.
28. Heilig Grab.
29. Augustinez Closter.
30. S. Michael.
31. S. Margretha.
32. S. Aurelia.
33. Deutsch Hauß.
34. Weyß thurn.
35. Cronenburger thor.
36. Juden thor.
37. S. Clara Werth.
38. Fischer thor.
39. Weyßtrein.
40. Spital Mühl.

26. Strasbourg, 1653.

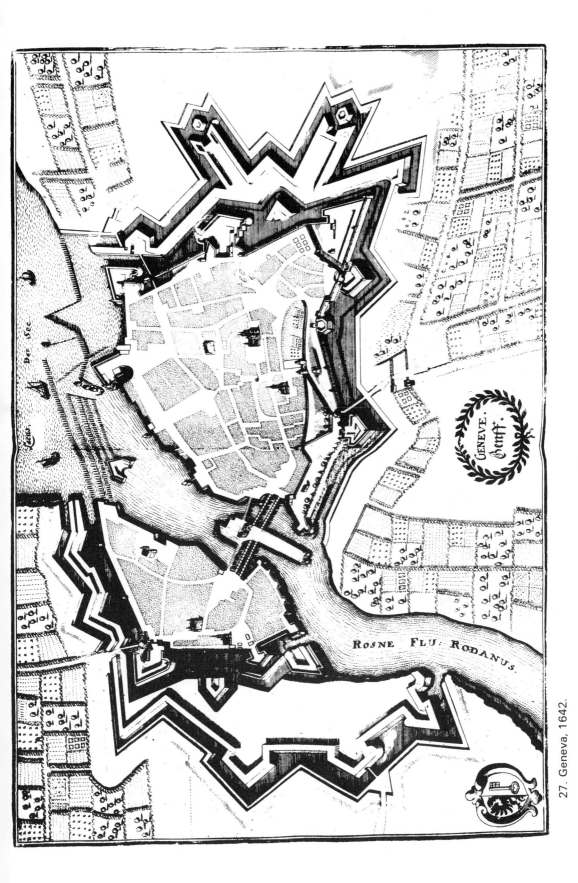

Der See.

Leman.

GENEVE.
Genff.

ROSNE FLU: RODANUS.

27. Geneva, 1642.

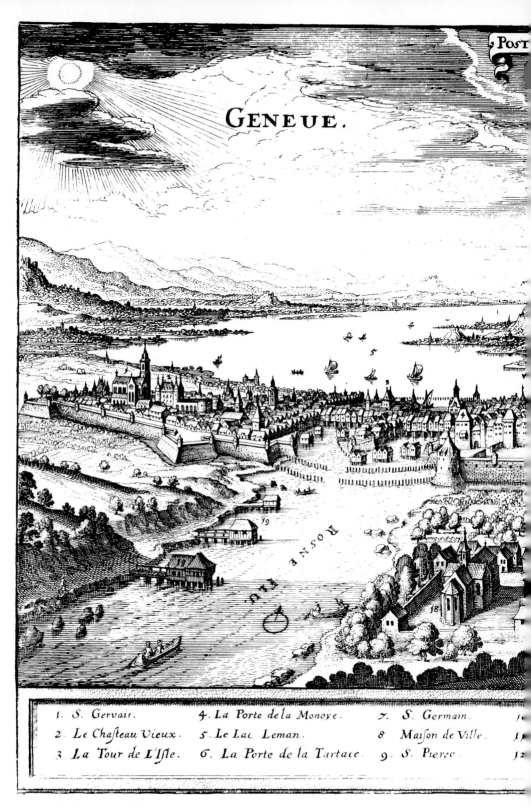

GENEUE.

1. S. Gervais.   4. La Porte de la Monoye.   7. S. Germain.   1ᵉ
2. Le Chasteau Vieux.   5. Le Lac Leman.   8. Maison de Ville.   1
3. La Tour de L'Isle.   6. La Porte de la Tartace.   9. S. Pierre.   1

28. Geneva, 1642.

POST NEBRAS LVX

Genff.

a Porte de Treille.	13. Bouleuerd du Pin	16. La Porte Neufue.	19. Moulins.
risons.	14. Bouleuerd de S. Legier	17. Bouleuerd de L'oye.	
Hospitale.	15. Porte de S Legier.	18. L'Hospitale.	

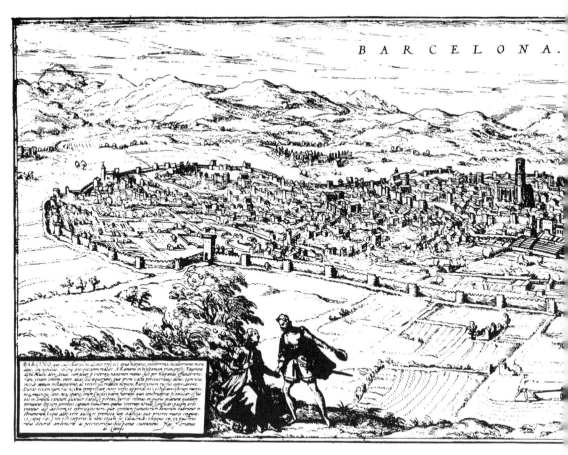

29. Barcelona (Braun and Hogenberg), 1574.

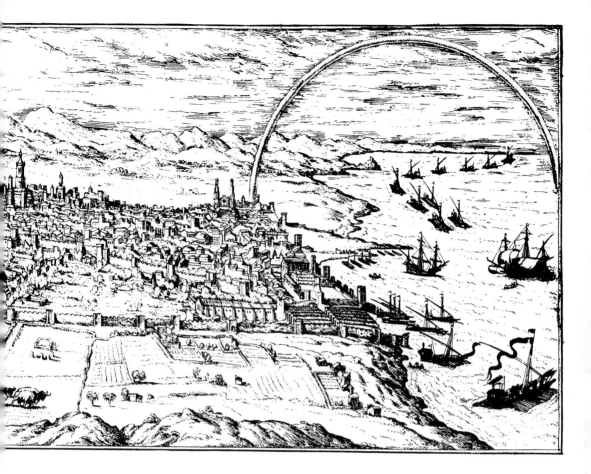

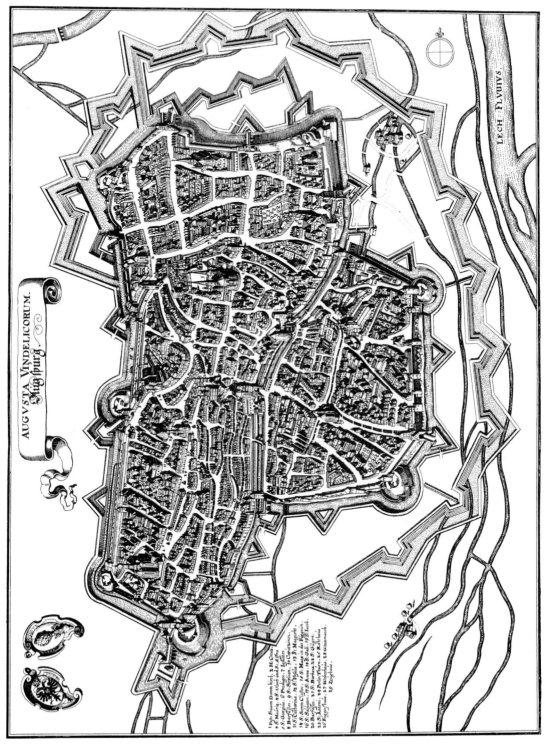

AVGVSTA VINDELICORVM. *Augspurg.*

LECH FLVVIVS.

1 *Vnfer Frawen Dom kirch.* 2 H. Creus.
3 *S: Moriz.* 4 *S: Vlrich vnd S: Affra.*
5 *S: Georgius.* 6 *S: Predigen.* 7 *Lgfstten.*
8 *Barsfsser.* 9 *S: Stephan.* 10 *Capucinaeter.*
11 *S: Katharina.* 12 *S: Vrsula.* 13 *B: Magget.*
14 *S: Servn Clofter.* 15 *S: Mang in der Fuggerin.*
16 *S: Salvator.* 17 *S: Anna.* 18 *S: Gall.* 19 *S: Iacob.*
20 *Barfsser.* 21 *S: Barbara.* 22 *S: Gilgen.*
23 *S: Adam.* 24 *Prim: Clofter.* 25 *Rathhaus.*
26 *Fuggerifhaus.* 27 *Kohterhaus.* 28 *Weinmarck.*
29 *Zeughaus.*

30. Augsburg, 1643.

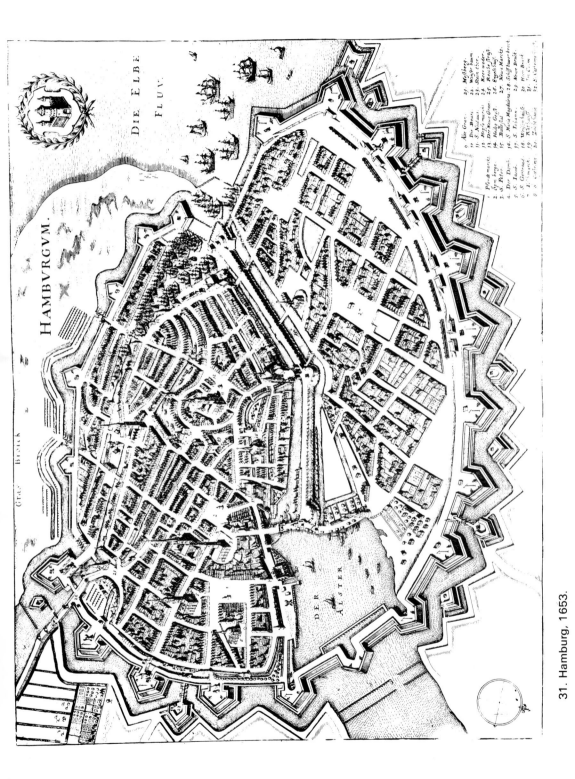

HAMBVRGVM.

DIE ELBE
FLUV.

GRAS BROCK

DER
ASTER

Pferd-marckt.
1. Nÿm kerge
2. S. Peter
3. Der Dom
4. S. Jacob
5. S. Gertraud
6. S. Iohan
7. S. Marien
8. S. Catharina
9. Alte Grav.
10. Die Brau.
11. S. Nidaui
12. Fugl-marckt
13. Die Neu Grav.
14. Holtz Graß
15. Ball-hauß
16. S. Maria Magdalena
17. S. Triann.
18. Waÿsenhauß
19. Kraj-gaß
20. Zuchthauß
21. Meßberg
22. Wajer baum
23. Stein thor
24. Kremerbal
25. Reich-Strafß
26. Engehhul
27. Neue Marckt
28. Schiff-hauer-brock
29. Noue Brock
30. Hoe Brock
31. In Cam
32. S. Lichrecht

31. Hamburg, 1653.

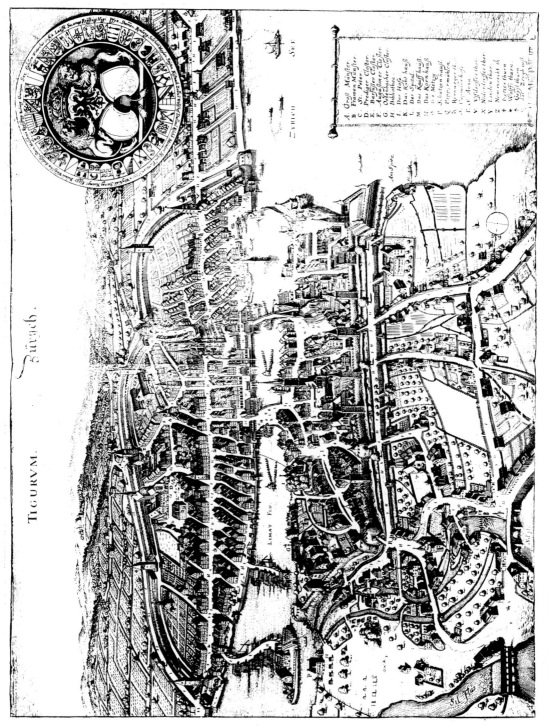

32. Zürich, 1642.

REIMS EN CHAMPAGNE

33. Reims, 1655.

Trier.

Treveris.

Mons Martis

Mosella Flu.

Apollinis mons

34. Trier, 1646.

35. Heilbronn, 1643.

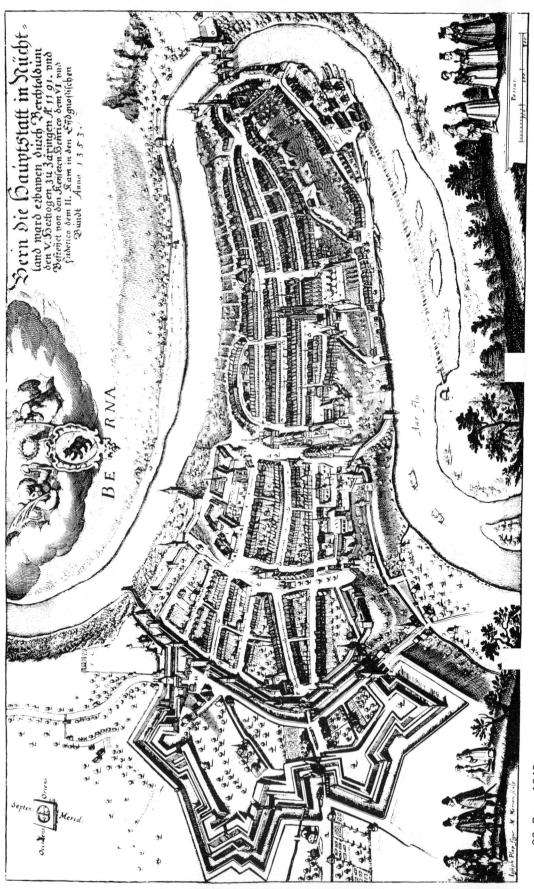

BERNA

Aar flu

Septen. Oriens Merid.

Passus. 100 200

36. Bern, 1642.

37. Ulm, 1643.

Sachsenhausen.

Francfurt.

FRANCOFURTUM UT
UERSUS ORIENTEM UISITUR.
Die Steinerne Brücke zu
Franckfurt wie selbige gegen
Auffgang gesehen wirdt.

M. Merian Sen.
fecit 1646.

A. Der Weinmarckt.
B. Der Mayn fluß.
C. Die Fahr port.
D. Leonharts port.

E. Metzger port.
F. Spittal.
G. Brücken thürn.
H. Leonharts thurn.

I. Heilig Geist Kirch.
K. S. Leonharts Stifft.
L. S. Bartolomei Stifft.
M. S. Nicolai Kirch.

N. Der untere Gran.
O. Der ober Gran.
P. Cletsche hoff.
Q. H. Drei Königs.

R. Deütsche Hauße.
S. Schau mayn port.
T. Neue Brücken mühl.
V. Offenbach.

38. Frankfurt am Main, 1646. Stone Bridge connects with
Sachsenhausen suburb.

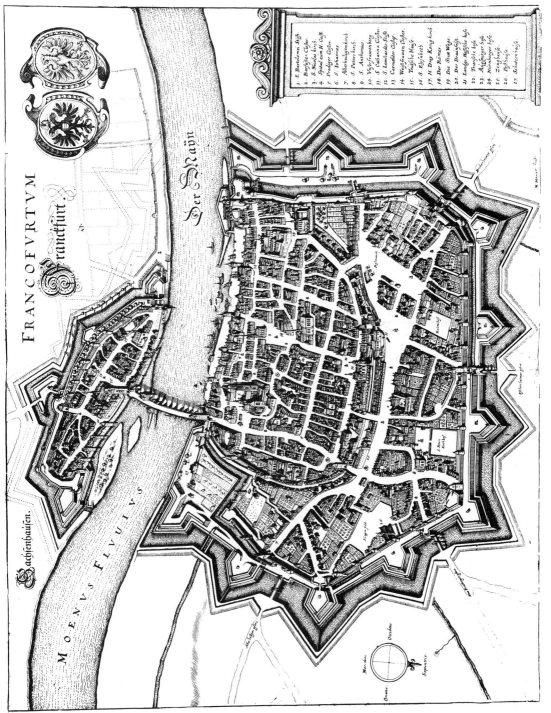

FRANCOFVRTVM
Franckfurt.

Der Mayn

Sachsenhausen.

MOENVS FLVVIVS

39. Frankfurt am Main, 1646.

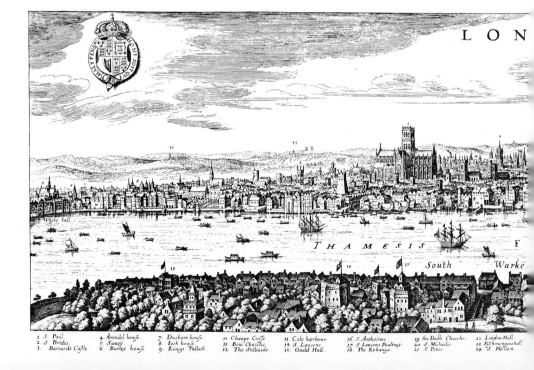

LON

Whyte hall

THAMESIS F

South Warke

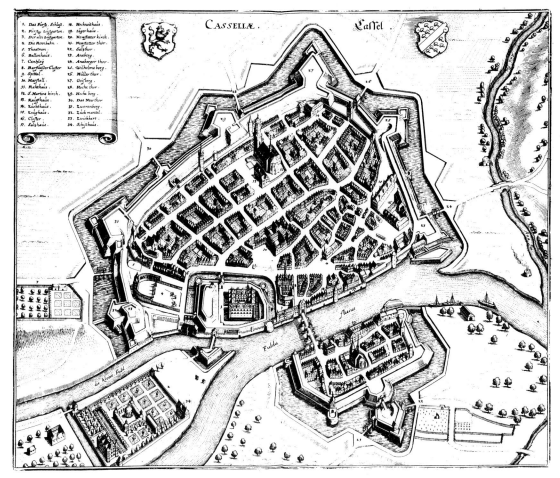

40. Kassel, c. 1646, with Unterneustadt (New Town) below.

41. London, view from Southwark, c. 1630–1640.

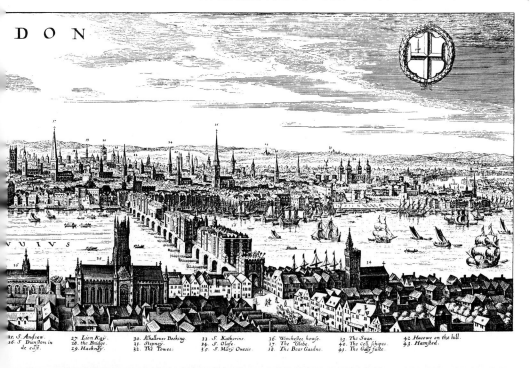

42. Cologne, 1646.

43. Goslar, Peterstrasse.

44. Rome, Piazza del Popolo, Tempesta view, 1593.

1 S. Schild
2 Rathhaus
3 Prediger Clost
4 Unser Frauen
5 Augustiner Cl.
6 S. Ægidy
7 Spital
8 Barfusel
9 S. Egidien Cl.
10 S. Laurentz
11 S. Jacobi
12 Carthaus Cl.

13 S. Clara Closter
14 S. Margareth Cl.
15 Zeughaus
16 Wasserthurn
17 Tragschhaus
18 Roßmarckt
19 Fischbach
20 Der Marckt
21 Der geschorn
22 Frauen thor
23 Schutthurn
24 Carlhaus Cl.

25 Das Schloß
26 Kornhaus
27 Lugersland
28 Ochsenfelder
29 Heumarckt
30 Neu thor
31 Haller thorlein
32 Spital thor
33 Frauen thor
34 Weiter thorlein
35 Lauffer thor
36 Die Vogtei

37 Thiergartner Hof
38 Fleisch Bruck
39 Kornmarckt
40 Marsfeld
41 Haller muhl
42 Hallleweiten
43 Muhlen
44 Straßen
45 Weiter thorlein
46 die Vestschleusen

MONACHIVM.
München.
Iser flu.
H Geist Anger.
16
20
32
1. Vnser Frawen Hauptkirch.
2. S. Peters Pfarrkirch.
3. Iesuiter Collegium vnd kirch.
4. H. Geist Spital.
5. Augustiner Closter
6. Barfusser Closter.
7. Vns. Frawen Gottsacker.
8. Capuciner Closter.
9. S. Peters Gottsacker.
10. S. Iacobs Frawen Closter.
11. S. Sebastian Capel.
12. S. Niclaus kirch.
13. New Stifft kirch
14. S. Sebastian kirch.
15. S. Anna kirch.
16. Chur Furstlich Palatium.
17. ChurFurstl. Lustgarten.
18. Zeughauser.
19. Hertzog Alberti Palatium.
20. Alten Hoff.
21. Herr von Preysing behausung.
22. Statt Rahthaus.
23. Landschafft haus
24. Der Schone thurn.
25. Der Marckt
26. Iser thor.
27. Sendlinger thor
28. Schiffer thor
29. Anger thor
30. Wurtzer thor.
31. Schwabinger thor.

46. Munich, 1644. Alter Hof at no. 20. Neue Residenz at no. 16. Neuhauserstrasse at no. 32.

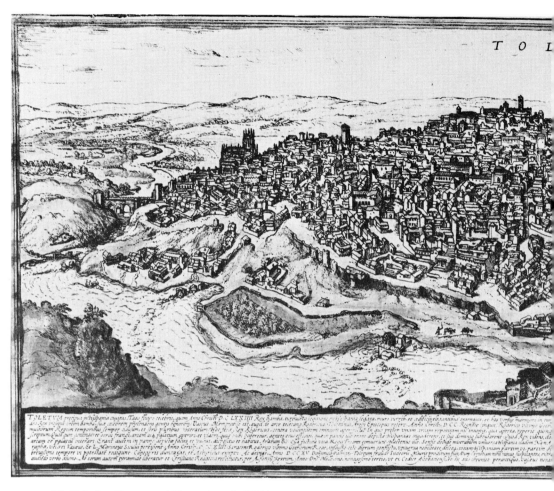

TOLETVM praecipua in hispania civitas.Tao fluvio celebri, quam Anno Christi D C LXXIIII Rex Bamba, turpiusta (equitur, velut banca legara, muro turrib. et aedificiis sumtibus exornavit, et has versus marmori in tu arca.Rex insignis urbem bamba sua celebrem p̄stinans pontis renovem. Vasquis Miremp̄so is est, juxta te arce tele tang Roderivus Toletinus, huic Episcopus refert. Anno Christi D CC Rogodie inquit. Rodericus vltimus visen.
multorum Regum temporibus semper adictum, et serio p̄cibus vocitatur, hic fecit. Rex Rodericus contra voluntatem omnium aperuit. In quo prefer vnam imam repositam in vincire, quo aperias reperis quem deprecum. Quid cum voluisset serio frangi.arcam alig, placitum agerent.et vacare, quid velit, superetur, agentes eius efficiunt, aut in pariet ille terni deprile hispanias nunc occupare,et his dominis subvenerunt. Quid Rex videns, do arcam et palatia viserari. Erant autem in turri, deip̄da facies et bruma, adspectu et natura, Arabum 80. Qua pictura visa Rex Roderivus conturbari, intelerins alio. Septic dictus miserabilem vmbram.hispania radem Nam A rapta, et,vri Vascus, & L. Marineus Siculus perhibent, Anno Christi D CC XLIII Saracenorum Rosae, insolito bello derum confusa, vyngorua nobilitate,delea totam hispaniam,tu partim Saracenorum
percussima tempore in potestate reaiqum Caetperis dominaxat, et litigious excepta. Ac demm. Anno D CC XV Damyni Palma-Toletum fraude Tutoris Mauris prodition fuit,Dum Tritium nimis suboptantes, rerire auferio verbo domino. Ac torum autem piramidi liberatur et Christiani Regalis restituitur, per Amonis Superim. Anno Dn̄i M.C.Ferino, nonagesimo tertio, et ex Codice Alcobaciensi,et ex suis etenim pervasitunt.Cujus
novis

47. Toledo (Braun and Hogenberg), 1574.

48. Tübingen, Plan 1819–1821.

dem Graben

nach Stuttgart

Rübenloch

Lange

Frosch = Gasse

im Nonnengässle

Gasse

Mezger = Gasse

Neue Strasse. Insmauer Thor

Convict

Neue

Hafen = Gasse

Hirsch = Gasse

beim Collegio

Strasse

Gasse hinter dem Pfloghof

Kirch = Gasse

Hafenmarkt

unter der Krone

Münz = Gasse

Neckar = Gasse

Neckar Thor

unter der Burſch

NECKAR

der kleine Wörth.

49. Tübingen, Market and Rathaus (site purchased 1433). Building
dates from late 15th century with later alterations.

50. Air view of Tübingen market, with Rathaus at lower left.

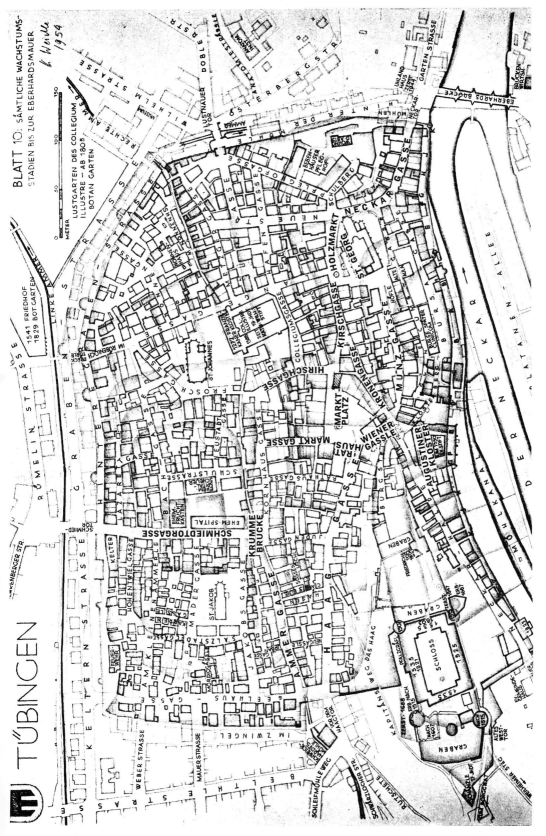

51. Tübingen, Weidle Plan 1954.

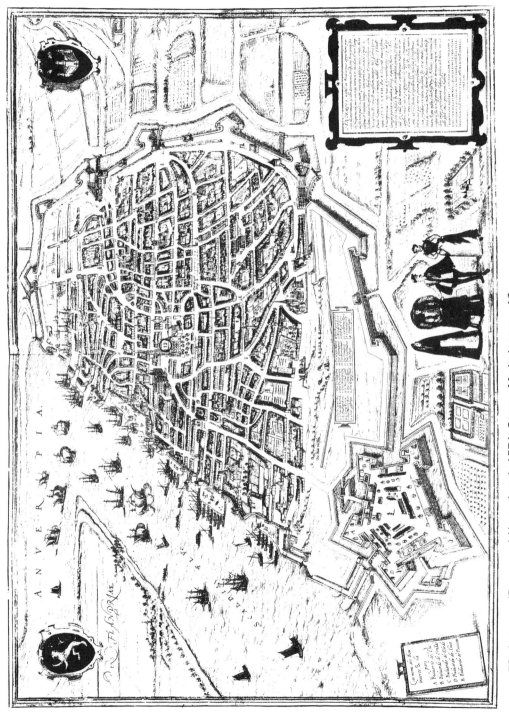

52. Antwerp (Braun and Hogenberg), 1574. Groote Markt is at no. 13.

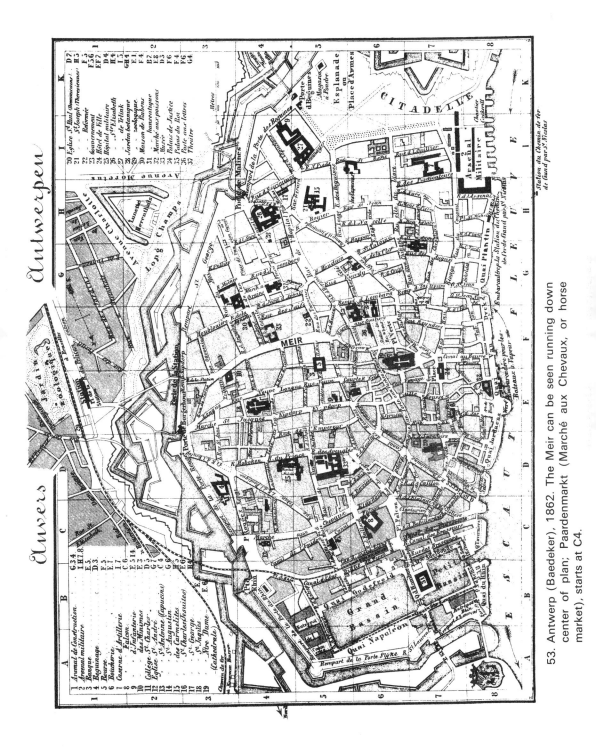

53. Antwerp (Baedeker), 1862. The Meir can be seen running down center of plan; Paardenmarkt (Marché aux Chevaux, or horse market), starts at C4.

Veduta della Badia Fiorentina, e del Palazzo del Potestà presa dalla Piazza della Chiesa de PP dell' Oratorio.

54. Florence, Bargello, Zocchi view, c. 1754.

55. Florence, Piazza del Duomo, 1733.

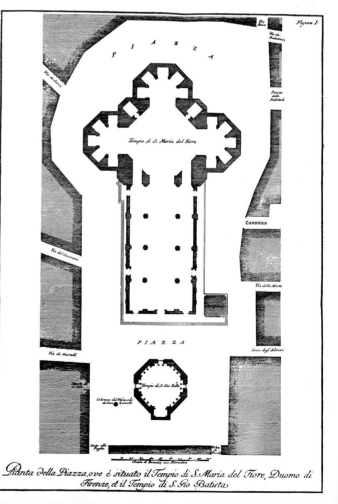

Pianta della Piazza, ove é situato il Tempio di S. Maria del Fiore, Duomo di Firenze, et il Tempio di S. Gio. Batista.

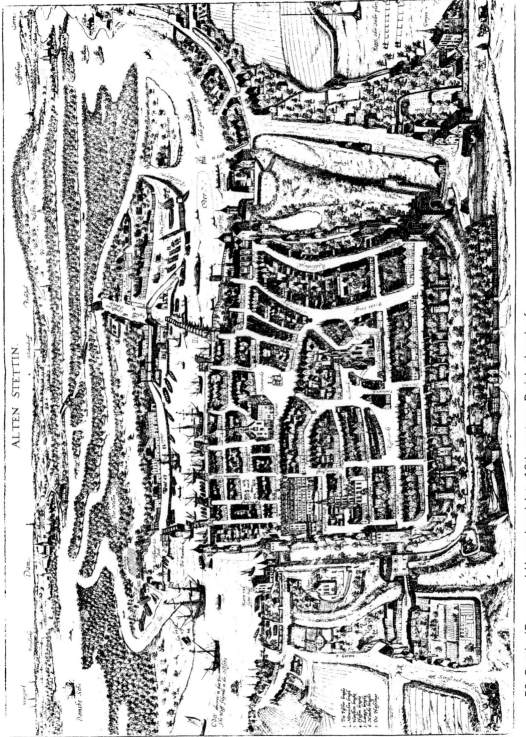

56. Stettin (Braun and Hogenberg) late 16th century. Parish church of St. Jacob with adjoining markets is in lower center, church with cemetery at lower right.

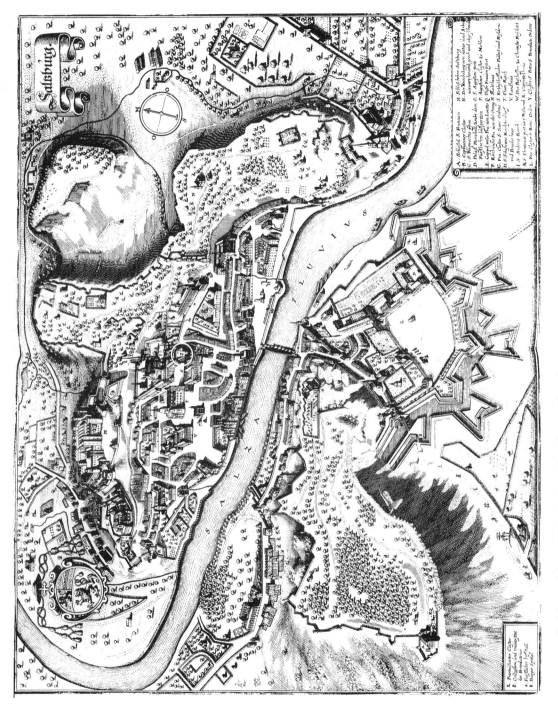

57. Salzburg, 1644. "Z" indicates Franciscan Church.

Wahre Contrafactur der Churfürstlichen Residentz Statt Heidelberg.

HEIDELBERGA.

Gaißberg

NECCAR FLUVIUS

58. Heidelberg, 1645.

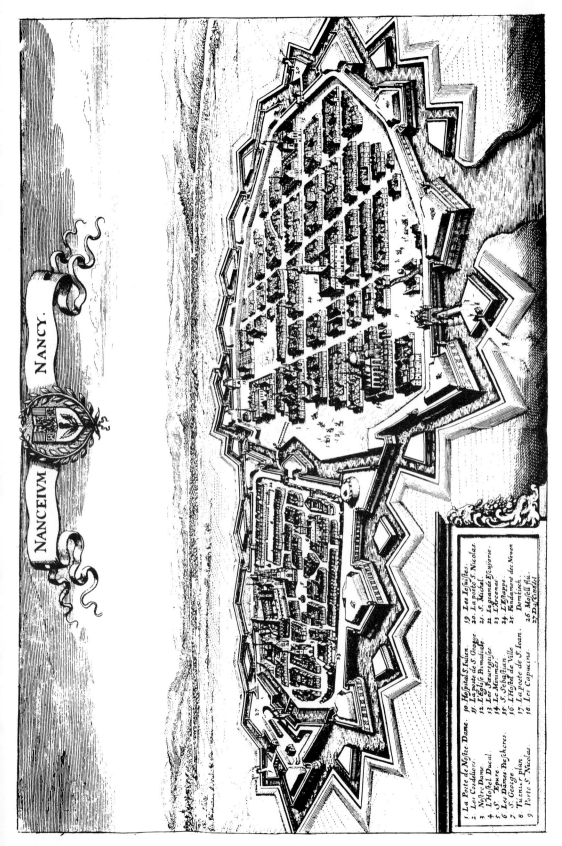

NANCEIVM NANCY.

1. La Poste de Nostre Dame.
2. Les Cordeliers.
3. Nostre Dame.
4. L'Hostel Ducal.
5. S. Epure.
6. Les Dames Preschores.
7. S. George.
8. Trenu. plan.
9. Porte S. Nicolas.
10. Hospital S. Iulien.
11. La porte de S. Gorge.
12. L'Eglise Parmatiale.
13. Les Iesuirguifer.
14. Le Minimer.
15. S. Sebastian.
16. L'Hostel de Ville.
17. La porte de S. Iean.
18. Les Capucins.
19. Les Iesuites.
20. La porte S. Nicolas.
21. S. Michel.
22. La grande Escuyerie.
23. L'Arcenac.
24. L'Escarpe.
25. Fondament des Neuen Domkiech.
26. Mosell fla.
27. Da Citadil.

59. Nancy, 1645.

Die Fürst. Statt
Stuetgart.

Der See

A. Das Fürstliche Schloß. B. Der
Fürstl. Stall. C. Die Cantzeley.
D. Der Fürstl. Lustgarten. E. Das
Newe Lusthauß. F. Alte Lusthauß.
G. Die Grotten vnd masserkunste.
H. Die Stiff Kirch. I. Das Rahts-
hauß. K. Spital Kirch.
L. Eßlinger Vorstatt. M. S. Leon-
hards Kirch.

60. Stuttgart, 1643.

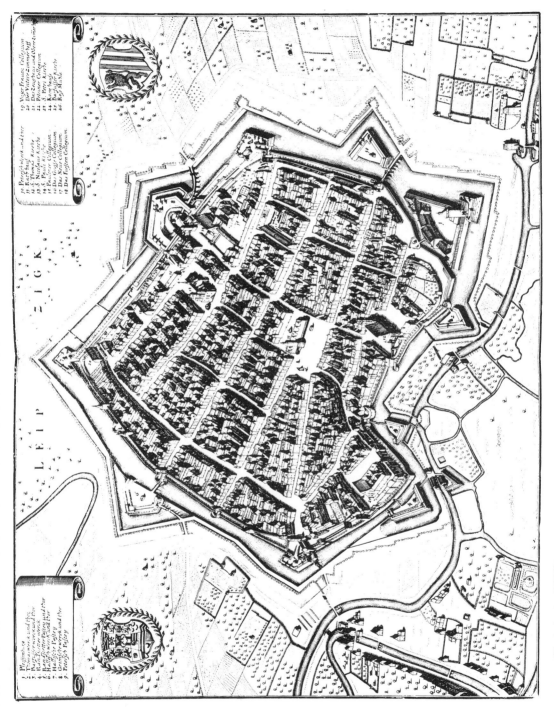

61. Leipzig, 1650.

INDEX OF CITIES

APPENDIX I   PLANNED CITIES

The colonial "new towns" which sprang up in the open country under the auspices of cities and princes in Italy, France, and Germany from the twelfth century on represent a phenomenon of "urban planning" rather different from the patterns of gradual organic development which have been the main concern of our discussion. They have been the subject of increasing attention in the literature and require further study, but the following points may be made:

The grid plans of the new towns, including main street markets and regular central squares, follow in the pattern of Roman colonial settlements, enough of which survived to serve as models. If the majority of medieval cities did not follow this pattern, it was due to the different social dynamics which determined their form, not to ignorance of the antique tradition. Planitz (in *Die deutsche Stadt im Mittelalter*, 2nd ed., Graz-Köln, 1965, pp. 94f.) is mistaken, I think, in assuming that the more or less triangular and wedge-shaped markets that are so widespread in medieval cities are also the result of planned layouts.

As a general phenomenon these planned towns are symptomatic of changing political and economic organization in Europe, leading first to regionalism (large areas economically and politically dependent on a dominant city) and then to national governments exploiting the economic resources of an entire country under absolute central control. In this sense they are more "Renaissance" than "medieval." While some of the early "new towns" were founded as trading centers (Freiburg i. Br., ca. 1120; Leipzig, ca. 1180 Fig. 61; and Lübeck, 1158), the purpose of most foundations after 1200 was mainly to assure political control of the surrounding non-urban areas. They were seldom wholly self-governing, but merely outposts of the central city. Many of the later "new towns" were slow in developing, and most of their major buildings date from the late fourteenth and fifteenth centuries (a point generally ignored). Mainly military bastions for the protection of the peasantry against the survivors of the landed aristocracy, their walls and bastions were the first thing to be built by the colonists. Major tax incentives, such as lifetime tax exemption on the houses to be built, in addition to free land for building, were necessary to induce the colonists to leave the central cities to populate these new towns. The trappings of real cities, the public buildings, churches, hospitals, etc. came later if at all.[22]

Rigidly planned and controlled from the beginning, few of these new towns had the potential of becoming independent cities, and hardly any of them achieved major importance in later times. Leipzig (Fig. 61) and Lübeck, in exceptionally favorable locations, and where the planned sector represents an addition to already existing settlements, are important exceptions; Freiburg i. Br., a foundation of the dukes of Zähringen, is a minor one. It may be worth investigating how far the rigid layout of these towns helped or hindered their development and their ultimate success or failure as cities.

APPENDIX II   BIBLIOGRAPHICAL NOTE

The literature dealing in one way or another with the medieval city is extensive. Its authors are almost without exception political, social, and economic historians concerned with the medieval city as an institution, not as an architectural form. This fact is not surprising since there is a tangible body of evidence in the form of charters, letters, contracts, laws, scientific treatises, chronicles, poems, coins, and a variety of common and artistic objects on which their observations are based. Tangible evidence for the form of medieval cities and their gradual evolution in the crucial period before about 1200, on the other hand, is much scarcer. In the case of medieval cities whose origins go back to Roman frontier camps, it is usually evident that the regular outlines of the Roman plan survived as the core of the growing medieval city. But this does not explain the quite different character of the post-antique additions to these towns or of post-antique cities in general. The same, on the whole, may be said of the literature on antique cities. While the regular town plans of the Hellenistic and Roman periods have attracted attention, only a beginning has been made in the analysis of the not uncommon irregular towns of antiquity (cf. R. Martin, *L'Urbanisme dans la Grèce Antique*, Paris, 1956).

While most scholars have avoided the problem, "town planners" and art historians with an ideological axe to grind have been analyzing medieval cities in order to deduce the artistic principles by which they were presumably built, since the days of Camillo Sitte (*Der Städtebau nach seinen künstlerischen Grundsätzen*, Vienna, 1889; English transl. by G. R. and C. C. Collins, *City Planning according to Artistic Principles*, New York, 1965). Both disciples and critics of Sitte followed this approach, sketching detail plans of parts of cities (streets, intersections, plazas, etc.) and analyzing the visual impressions created by various arrangements. A recent example of this school is W. Rauda, *Raumprobleme im europäischen Städtebau*, Munich, 1956. (Cf. G. R. Collins, *Camillo Sitte and the Birth of Modern City Planning*, New York, 1965, p. 135, n. 95.)

APPENDIX III   BIBLIOGRAPHY

This bibliography is a brief guide to the essential literature dealing with the political, social, and economic background of medieval cities and related problems. For a general up-to-date review see *The Cambridge Economic History of Europe*, M. Postan et al., eds., Cambridge (England), Vol. II, 1952; III, 1963, including extensive additional bibliography.

THE ANTIQUE BACKGROUND

Charlesworth, M. P., *Trade Routes and Commerce of the Roman Empire*, 2nd ed., Cambridge, 1926.

Frank, T., *Economic History of Rome*, 2nd ed. Baltimore, 1927.

Frank, T., *Economic Survey of Ancient Rome*, 5 vols., Baltimore, 1933–1940.

Rostovtzeff, M., *The Social and Economic History of the Hellenistic World*, 3 vols., Oxford, 1941.

Rostovtzeff, M., *Social and Economic History of the Roman Empire*, Oxford, 1926.

Walbank, F. W., "Trade and Industry under the Late Roman Empire in the West," *Cambridge Economic History of Europe*, II, 1952, pp. 33f. Good summary of major problems.

Ward-Perkins, J. B., "Early Roman Towns in Italy," *Town Planning Review*, XXVI, 1955–1956, pp. 127–154. See also his forthcoming *Cities of Ancient Greece and Italy* in this series.

THE END OF ANTIQUITY

Dopsch, A., *Wirtschaftliche und soziale Grundlagen der europäischen Kulturentwicklung aus der Zeit von Cäsar bis auf Karl den Grossen*, 2 vols., 1st ed., 1918–1924.

Lot, F., *La fin du monde antique et le début du moyen âge*, Paris, 1927.

Pirenne, H., *Mahomet et Charlemagne*, Paris, 1937; English ed.: *Mohammed and Charlemagne*, Meridian Books, New York, 1957.

CAROLINGIAN PROBLEMS

Bloch, M., "Le Problème de l'Or au Moyen Âge," *Annales d'Histoire Sociale et Économique*, V, 1933.

Dopsch, A., *Die Wirtschaftsentwicklung der Karolingerzeit*, 2 vols., 2nd ed., Weimar, 1922.

Grierson, P., "Money and Coinage under Charlemagne," *Karl der Grosse, Lebenswerk und Nachleben*, W. Braunfels, gen. ed., I, Düsseldorf, 1965, pp. 501–536.

Pirenne, H., *Economic and Social History of Medieval Europe*, (English transl.), London, 1936.

CRITIQUE OF PIRENNE'S POSITION

Lopez, R. S., "Mohammed and Charlemagne: a revision," *Speculum*, XVIII, 1943, pp. 14–38.

Mundy, J. H., Introduction to H. Pirenne, *Early Democracies in the Low Countries*, New York, 1963.

Postan, M., and R. S. Lopez, "The Trade of Medieval Europe," *Cambridge Economic History of Europe*, II, 1952, pp. 119ff.

MEDIEVAL CITIES AND THEIR ORIGINS

Ennen, E., *Frühgeschichte der europäischen Stadt*, Bonn, 1953.

Mundy, J. H. and P. Riesenberg, *The Medieval Town*, Princeton, 1958.

Petit-Dutaillis, C., *Les communes, caractères et évolution des origines au XVIIIe siècle*, Paris, 1947.

Pirenne, H., *Medieval Cities, their Origins and the Revival of Trade*, Princeton, 1925; New York, 1956.

Rörig, F., *Die europäische Stadt und die Kultur des Bürgertums im Mittelalter*, Göttingen, 1955.

BELGIUM: Vercauteren, F., *Étude sur les* civitates *de la Belgique Seconde*, Brussels, 1934.

ENGLAND: *Borough and Town. A study of urban origins in England*, Cambridge, Mass., 1933.

FRANCE: Ganshof, F. L., *Étude sur le développement des villes entre Loire et Rhin au moyen âge*, Paris-Brussels, 1944.

GERMANY: Planitz, H., *Die deutsche Stadt im Mittelalter*, 2nd ed., Graz-Köln, 1965.

ITALY: Mengozzi, G., *La città italiana nell alto medio evo*, 2nd ed., Florence, 1931.

Braunfels, W., *Mittelalterliche Stadtbaukunst in der Toskana*, Berlin, 1953.

SPAIN: Balbas, L. Torres, "La Edad Media," *Resumen historico del Urbanismo en España*, Madrid, 1954.

Jurgens, O., *Spanische Städte. Ihre bauliche Entwicklung und Ausgestaltung*, Hamburg, 1926.

RECENT STUDIES ON MEDIEVAL CITIES IN EUROPE: Institut für geschichtliche Landesforschung des Bodenseegebietes in Konstanz, *Studien zu den Anfängen des europäischen Städtewesens*. Vorträge und Forschungen, IV. Lindau-Constance, 1958.

ILLUSTRATED SURVEY OF MEDIEVAL CITIES: Gutkind, E. A., *Urban Development in Central Europe*, London, 1964; and later volumes in Gutkind's *International History of City Development*.

PARISH AND TOWN DEVELOPMENT: Friedmann, A., *Paris, ses rues, ses paroisses du moyen âge à la Révolution. Origine et évolution des circonscriptions paroissiales*, Paris, 1959.

POPULATION IN MEDIEVAL CITIES: Lot, F., *Recherches sur la population et la superficie des cités remontant à l'époque gallo-romaine*, 2 vols., Paris, 1944–46, 1950.

TOWN PLANNING AND MEDIEVAL CITIES

Brinckmann, A. E. *Stadtbaukunst, Geschichtliche Querschnitte und neuzeitliche Ziele*, Berlin-Neubabelsberg, 2nd ed., 1922.

Sitte, C., (see bibliographic note at end of Appendix II.)

Zucker, P., *Town and Square from the Agora to the Village Green*, New York, 1959.

TOPOGRAPHICAL SOURCES FOR THE STUDY OF MEDIEVAL CITIES

Braun, Georg, and Hogenberg, Franz, *Beschreibung und Contrafactur der vornembster Stät der Welt*, 1574. (Facsimile ed., Verlag Müller & Schindler, Plochingen, 1965).

Hollar, Wenzel: H. Appel, *Wenzel Hollar in Düren. Die topographischen Darstellungen Dürens bis zum Jahr 1664*, 1957; A. M. Hind, *Wenceslaus Hollar*, London 1922.

Merian, Mattheus: Merian Europa, Bärenreiter Verlag, Kassel, 1965. All of the original topographical volumes with plates by Mattheus and Caspar Merian and with texts by Martin Zeiler have been republished since 1961 in facsimile volumes by the Bärenreiter Verlag, Kassel.

Topographical monographs on individual cities usually include reproductions of various early plans and views.

NOTES

1. F. W. Walbank, "Trade and Industry under the Later Roman Empire in the West," *Cambridge Economic History of Europe*, II, 1952, pp. 33ff. gives a recent scholarly view of the problems confronting the Roman state in its last centuries.

2. A survey of recent studies in this field may be found in the *Cambridge Economic History of Europe*, Vol. II, 1952 and Vol. III, 1963.

3. H. Planitz, *Die Deutsche Stadt im Mittelalter*, 2nd ed., Graz-Köln, 1965, pp. 35ff.

4. H. Saalman, *Medieval Architecture*, New York, 1962, pp. 14ff.

5. The bullion acquired was minted in monastery mints and the coins were used to further the chief economic goal which the monasteries held in common with all feudal domains: self-suffiency through the acquisition of additional domain lands. Monasteries as mint owners: *Cambridge Economic History of Europe*, III, 1963, p. 581, as money lenders: ibid., pp. 440ff.

6. Concerning the continuity of antique architectural forms in medieval and Renaissance cities, cf. A. Boethius, *The Golden House of Nero: Some Aspects of Roman Architecture*, Ann Arbor, Mich., 1960.

7. An important step in the direction of such knowledge has been made by the Abbé Adrien Friedmann in his study *Paris, ses rues, ses paroisses du moyen âge à la Révolution. Origine et évolution des circonscriptions paroissiales*, Paris, 1959.

8. Cf. E. A. Gutkind, *Urban Development in Central Europe*, London, 1964, App. IV, "Residential Strongholds for Local Magnates," for such towers in Germany. Many of them survive in Italian cities.

9. K. Weidle, *Die Entstehung von Alt-Tübingen*, Tübingen, 1955.

10. Originally the Kirchgasse opening was only half as wide. Cf. Weidle, *op. cit.*, p. 50.

11. See W. Braunfels, *Mittelalterliche Stadtbaukunst in der Toskana*, Berlin 1953.

12. R. Davidsohn, *Geschichte von Florenz*, I–IV, Berlin, 1896–1927.

13. Concerning guilds, cf. S. L. Thrupp, "The Guilds" in the *Cambridge Economic History of Europe*, III, 1963, pp. 230ff. with extensive bibliography.

14. Cf. Saalman, *Medieval Architecture*, p. 40.

15. Cf. Friedmann, *op. cit.*

16. The history of Christian monasticism begins in late antiquity in the Christian East where its characteristic form was that of a hermitic life spent in isolated and ascetic devotion. A number of monks might live in proximity to an important holy site or around a martyr's church, but each one isolated himself in his individual little hut, joining occasionally with the others in common prayer. Western monasticism as initiated under St. Benedict, on the other hand, was coenobitic, i.e., characterized by a regulated life in a monastery where the brothers lived together, sometimes in common dormitories, sometimes in individual cells under a common roof under the supervision of an elected abbot (whence such monasteries are called "abbeys"). The *regula* or rule determined the activities of every waking and sleeping hour. Benedict's rule enjoined the brothers *laborare et orare* (to work and to pray). Isolation from and independence of the secular world was the goal of the Benedictines. Their abbeys became oases of learning (copying of ancient and contemporary books to enlarge the monastery libraries was a major task). Economic self-

sufficiency was attained by producing food, wine, medicine, garments, parchment, etc. on their own lands and in their own workshops (cf. the Plan of St. Gall, Fig. 4, our earliest and most important plan of such a monastery). But the very autonomy of the individual abbeys made them an easy target for political penetration by their aristocratic patrons and founders. The sons of kings were educated in the abbeys. The abbots were frequently members of the royal family. The abbeys were instruments of Carolingian policy as much as places of retreat from the world.

From the late eighth century onward Benedictine monasticism underwent numerous internal changes leading to the branching off of various reformed orders. Since dependence on secular patrons tended to lead to secularization of monastic life, the new orders attempted to avoid secular patronage that had "strings attached" and to shift their allegiance to the papacy in Rome, whose power was gradually increasing. The monastic emphasis changed from economic self-sufficiency involving secular possessions, occupations and commitments (although these could never be wholly avoided) to study and prayer, and from the absolute but easily corrupted autonomy of each monastery under its all-powerful abbot to centralized international control under an even more powerful (and hence less easily seduced) general abbot (the Cluniac reform movement). The Cistercians under the dramatic leadership of St. Bernard of Clairvaux, coming to the peak of their influence in the twelfth century as the rigid patterns of feudal social and political organization were beginning to dissolve, preached renewed purity, abstinence, and dedication to Christian ideals in monasteries located away from urban centers, frequently pioneer communities engaged in clearing and cultivating virgin lands.

Common to all these orders was a regulated life within the confines of the monastery. But the spiritual and material problems and challenges presented by the rapidly increasing and often heretical populations in the cities could not be solved in the traditional monasteries. They had to be met in the cities by an entirely new kind of monk living a dedicated life in an entirely new way. The numerous orders which sprang up in response to this challenge, founded by St. Francis, St. Dominic and others in the late twelfth and early thirteenth centuries, had numerous traits in common. What was needed was not isolation from the world, but intense involvement in it. What more logical way to achieve this involvement than by ordering the brothers not to work but to *beg* for their living (lat. *mendicare*, to beg; hence the "mendicant orders") ! Clad in rough brown or white cloth, a rope for a belt, simple sandals on their feet instead of leather shoes (some orders even went barefoot), the mendicant brothers were living embodiments of Christian humility, consciously identifying with the poor and downtrodden who were the main object of their attention. They helped those who could give by providing the occasion for a charitable act, kept a minimum for their bare necessities, and shared the rest with the poor. Their convents were in the peripheries of the city, where the poor were concentrated and could be gathered in the great barnlike churches of the orders for fire-and-brimstone exhortation—but the main mission of the mendicants was outside the cloister walls, which they left daily, to return only for prayer and sleep.

The problems of social control were complex, however. Those who could not be brought to the orthodox faith by a helping hand and vigorous exhortation were brought to it by force, for the Pope had entrusted these orders with the task of the Inquisition, giving them power of life and death over heretics, a power used with great effect in the thirteenth and fourteenth centuries. Close to the turbulent masses, the monks knew everything that was going on, giving help where it was needed, arresting rebellion and heresy where it sprang up.

120

As the power of the cities waned, the mendicant orders declined as well. With the rise of national states (and national heresy: the Hussite rebellion and the German, Dutch and English Reformation) a new monastic operation—on a high level of national and international power—was needed. The great orders of the Counter Reformation with the Jesuits in the lead, were the response, and they played an important role in the survival of the Roman Catholic Church.

No organization once created ever disappears without a trace and the mendicant orders have survived to this day. The Inquisition is a thing of the past, but the brothers continue their works of charity and mercy in the great cities of our time.

17. R. Krautheimer, *Die Kirchen der Bettelorden in Deutschland*, Cologne, 1925.

18. The Franziskanerkirche in the center of Salzburg, a seeming exception to this pattern, was originally a parish church, given to the Franciscans in the sixteenth century (Fig. 57).

19. Cf. J. U. Nef, "Mining and Metallurgy in Medieval Civilisation," *Cambridge Economic History of Europe*, II, 1952, Section IX: "The Growth in the Authority of the Prince," pp. 480ff.

20. Gene A. Brucker, *Florentine Politics and Society*, 1343–1378, Princeton, 1962.

21. H. Saalman, "Tommaso Spinelli, Michelozzo, Manetti, and Rossellino," *Journal of the Society of Architectural Historians*, XXV, 1966, pp. 160ff. For an interesting comparison of late medieval and Renaissance views of Florence, cf. H. Baron, *The Crisis of the Early Italian Renaissance*, rev. ed., Princeton, 1966, pp. 202–203.

22. See M. Richter, "Die 'Terra Murata' im florentinischen Gebiet," *Mitteilungen des Kunsthistorischen Institutes in Florenz*, V, 1940, pp. 351ff. for a preliminary study of such towns in Tuscany.

INDEX

Napoleon, age of, 42
New towns *(bastides)*, 114
Normandy, 18
Normans, 18
North Sea, 18
Notaries, 41
Novi homines, 44
Nuremberg, 20; Gänsemarkt, 28; *Fig.* 45

Osservanti (Order of Observant Minor Friars), 40

Padua, University of, 41
Palaces, in late medieval towns, 44–45; *all' antico*, 45
Papacy, 18, 120n
Paris, 18, 21, 40; Carmelites, 40; Celestines, 40; Commercial center, 40; Cordeliers (Franciscans), 40; Faubourg St.-Paul, 40; Île de la Cité, 41; Jacobins (Dominicans), 40; Left Bank, 40, 41; Les Halles, 34–35; Louvre, 43; Place de Grève, 35; Place Maubert, 34; Porte de Bussy, 41; Prés aux clerks, 41; Right Bank, 40; Rue St. Denis, 35; Rue St. Jacques, 40; St. Jacques-le-Boucherie, 35; Servites, 40; University, 41; Wall of Philip Augustus, 35, 40; *Fig.* 7
Parish churches: boundaries, 39; role in medieval cities, 38–39
Peasants, in cities, 29, 31
Philip II Augustus, of France (1180–1223), building of Paris wall, ca. 1200, 35, 40
Pilgrims, in cities, 41
Pirenne, H., 15
Pisa, 18
Planitz, H., 114
Planned towns, 114
Platea, 32
Pompeii, *Fig.* 1
Population growth, in 12th–13th centuries, 26; epidemics due to, 41
Prisons: Le Stinche, Florence, 37
Production: Carolingian, 16; expansion in eleventh century, 18–19; location of, in medieval city, 28; Roman, 12, 13
Public buildings: location of, 21; scale of, 21

Quentovic (Holland), 18

Real estate values, in medieval city, 40
Renaissance, revival of rigid planning in, 18, 43
Regula, Benedictine, 119n; *see also* Benedictine order
Reims, *Fig.* 33
Religion, 12, 13
Rivers, in medieval cities, 22
Roman Cities, *see* Roman Empire

Roman Empire: agriculture, 12; apartment houses, 13; architecture, 13; army, 13; artisans, 5; barbarian invasions, 15; baths, 13; building materials, 13; circuses, 13; cities, 12; colonial towns, 29, 114; country houses, 12; decline of, 15; engineering, 13; languages, 13; law, 12; law courts, 12; living standard, 12; market place, 12; merchants, 13; mystery religions, 13; port facilities, 12; religion, 12, 13; road system, 12; secular life, 12; shore resorts, 13; storage terminals, 12; temples, 12, 13; theaters, 13; town planning, 16, 114; transportation, 12, 13; urbanization, degree of, 14
Rome: early views of, 21: Campo de' Fiori, 28; Forum of Trajan, 16; papacy, 18; *Figs.* 2, 44
Ruskin, John, 20
Russia, 18

Salzburg, Franziskanerkirche, 121n; *Fig.* 57
Sanitation, 41
Servites (Order of Servants of the Virgin Mary), 40; *see also* Mendicant orders
Seville, *Fig.* 21
Siena, Campo, 35
Spanish colonial towns, 29
St. Bernard of Clairvaux, 120n
St. Denis (Paris), Abbey of, 18
St. Dominic, Order of (Ordinis Predicatorum), 39, 120n
St. Francis, Order of (Ordinis Sancti Francisci), 39, 120n; *see also* Mendicant orders
St. Gall, plan of, 16, 17, 120n; *Fig.* 4
Ste.-Geneviève (Paris), Abbey of, 18
St. Germain-des-Prés (Paris), Abbey of, 18, 41
S. Maria del Fiore (Florence), 37; Porta della Canonica, 37
Stettin, 43; *Fig.* 56
Stinche (Prison), Florence, 37
Strasbourg, 20; *Fig.* 26
Streets: changing form of, 35; statutes governing, 30; definition of, 30; funnel formation, 31, 32; width of, 30
Street settlements, linear, 32
Stuttgart, 43; *Fig.* 60

Taxes: bridge tolls, 26; exemptions to settlers of "new towns," 114; gate taxes, 22, 25, 26; magnates' share of, 61
Textile industry, 43, 44
Toledo, *Fig.* 47
Towers: as residences in thirteenth century, 20, 31, 42; in town walls, 22; water towers, 22
Transportation: cost of, 13; mechanized, 13
Traveling players, 29
Trier, *Fig.* 34
Tübingen: Ammer River, 33; "Ammerstadt,"

33–34; Burg Hohentübingen, 33; *Collegium Illustre* (formerly Franciscan cloister), 33; as ducal residence city, 33; "Faules Eck," 33; Haaggasse, 34; Hirschgasse, 34; Holzmarkt, 33; Kirchgasse, 34; Kronengasse, 33; "Krumme Brücke," 34; Marktgasse, 44; Marktplatz, 32; Neckarhalde, 33; Neckar River, 33–34; "Neckarstadt," 33–34; Rathaus, 34; Stiftskirche St. Georg, 33; Wienergässle, 34; *Figs.* 48–51

Turks, 18

Tyrrhenian Sea, 18

Uberti, family (Florence), 37

Ulm, *Fig.* 37

Ulrich, Graf of Württemberg, 33; *see also* Tübingen

United States, South in 19th century, 12

Universities: role in medieval cities, 41; sites of, 41

Urban middle class, 44

Urban planning: Middle Ages, 114; planning statutes in medieval cities, 30; Renaissance, 29; Roman Empire, 12

Urban Proletariat, 39; in *faubourgs*, 40; political position in medieval cities, 44

Urban space: nature of, 28–35; penetrability of, 28

Urban upper class, 44; houses of, 44–45

Urbanization, 12, 13; patterns of, 21; planned, 29, 36, 114; revival of, 12, 13, 14, 16; stagnation of, 18

Venice: maritime role of, 18; patriciate, 44; Ruskin's view of, 20; *sottoportici*, 31

Vienna, Hofburg, 43; *Fig.* 14

Wagner, Richard, 20

Walls, 22–25; demolition of, 26, 31; dimensions, 23; enlargement, 23, 25; expenditures for, 23; in 16th–17th centuries, 26; used as habitations, 31

Weidle, K., 33, 34

Zähringen, Dukes of, 114

Zürich, *Fig.* 32

SOURCES OF ILLUSTRATIONS

The numbers following the sources correspond with figure numbers.

Baedeker, *Belgique et Hollande* (1862): 53

Courtesy Bärenreiter Verlag (Wilhelmshöhe, Germany): 5, 11, 13, 15, 17, 26, 30, 38, 41, 42, 57, 58, 59, 60, 61

Braun and Hogenberg, *Beschreibung und Contrafactur der vornembster Stät der Welt* (1574): 8, 21, 22, 25, 29, 47, 52; (1590): 23, 56

Courtesy Bolletino della commissione archeologica communale di Roma, Italy; MacDonald, *The Architecture of the Roman Empire*, Yale University Press (New Haven 1965): 2

Bürger- und Verkehrsverein, Tübingen: 50

Courtesy Dura-Europos Publications: 3

Foto-Walterbusch, Coesfeld, Westphalia: 43

Istituto Geografico Militare, Florence, Italy: 19

Munich Alte Pinakotek: 16

Nelli-Sgrilli: 55

Rossini, *Le Antichità di Pompei* (1830): 1

Howard Saalman: 7, 48

Stiftsbibliothek, St. Gallen, Switzerland: 4

Tempesta, *Romae Prospectus* (1593) (Schück Facsimile 1915): 44

Weidle, *Die Entstehung von Alt-Tübingen*, H. Laupp'sche Buchhandlung (Tübingen 1954): 51

Zeiller, *Topographiae* (1649): 6, 9, 10, 12, 14, 18, 24, 27, 28, 31, 32, 33, 34, 35, 36, 39, 40, 45, 46

Zocchi, *Scelta di XXIV vedute di Firenze* (1754): 20, 54